Graham Swift's
Last Orders

CONTINUUM CONTEMPORARIES

Also available in this series:

Forthcoming in this series:

· **GRAHAM SWIFT'S**

Last Orders

A READER'S GUIDE

PAMELA COOPER

CONTINUUM | NEW YORK | LONDON

2002

The Continuum International Publishing Group Inc
370 Lexington Avenue, New York, NY 10017

The Continuum International Publishing Group Ltd
The Tower Building, 11 York Road, London SE1 7NX

www.continuumbooks.com

Printed in the United States of America

Library of Congress Cataloging-in-Publication Data

Cooper, Pamela, 1955–
     Graham Swift's Last orders : a reader's guide / Pamela Cooper.
        p. cm. — (Continuum contemporaries)
     Includes bibliographical references.
     ISBN 0-8264-5242-6 (pbk. : alk. paper)
     1. Swift, Graham, 1949– Last orders. I. Title. II. Series.
PR6069.W47 L33 2002
823'.914—dc21
                                                              2001047833
     ISBN 0–8264–5242–6

Contents

The Novelist

BIOGRAPHY

Graham Swift was born in South London in 1949. His father, a civil servant, had been a naval pilot in World War II. Swift's earliest schooling was in South London and, in the late 1960s, he went to Cambridge University to study English Literature. Swift remembers wanting to be a writer from the age of twelve or thirteen. As a child he read a lot, and he traces his ambition to write from a powerful "sense of the word" which he developed in a home without television. After graduating from Cambridge in 1970, Swift received a grant to do a second degree at the University of York. Although he never completed his thesis, it was at York that he began to work seriously on his writing. After attending the University, Swift supported himself by doing a variety of jobs. The most important of these was part-time teaching at the Colleges of Further Education in London. He also worked, at different times, in a mental hospital and as a security guard.

In a 1998 interview, Swift recalls an arduous, fifteen-year apprenticeship in his craft before the publication of his first novel, *The Sweet-Shop Owner* in 1980. This was followed by *Shuttlecock* in 1981. Both novels were published initially by Allen Lane, and reissued within two or three years by Penguin. A collection of short stories, "Learning to Swim," was published in 1982 by London Magazine Editions. Many of the stories in this volume had appeared in publications like *London Magazine* and *Punch*, and in collections of short stories like *New Stories* and *Winter's Tales*. One of them, "Chemistry," had also been broadcast on BBC Radio 3. Swift's early fiction was well-received by critics and readers alike, but it was the publication of *Waterland* by William Heinemann in 1983 that solidified his reputation and popularity. After the success of this novel, which was later made into a film starring Jeremy Irons, Swift was able to give up teaching and has lived by his writing ever since. Before the publication of *Last Orders* by Picador in 1996, he wrote two other novels, *Out of this World* (Penguin, 1988) and *Ever After* (Pan Books, 1992).

Graham Swift has received numerous prizes for his writing. His second novel, *Shuttlecock*, received the Geoffrey Faber Memorial Prize. *Waterland* won the *Guardian* Fiction Award, the Winifred Holtby Memorial Prize, the Italian Permio Grinzane Cavour, and was short-listed for the highly prestigious Booker Prize. *Ever After* won the French Prix du Meilleur Livre Etranger, and *Last Orders* was awarded the Booker Prize in 1996. Swift enjoys an extensive international reputation; his work has been translated into more than twenty languages. In addition, a film version of *Last Orders* has recently been completed, directed by the Australian Fred Schepisi. Despite his fame, Swift maintains a low-profile as a writer, giving few interviews. He has said that while winning the Booker Prize has been "a delight," it has not changed his life. His hobby is fly-fishing and, in 1986, he edited, with David Profumo, an anthology of fishing in literature entitled *The Magic Wheel* (Heinemann). Graham Swift lives and works in London, with his long-time partner, the writer Candice Rodd, to whom many of his works are dedicated.

THEMATIC OVERVIEW

In a 1998 interview with Lewis Burke Frumkes for the journal *Writer*, Graham Swift was asked the following question: "What does water mean to you?" His reply was evocative. "I have kind of resisted the connection," he said, but went on to explain that for him water does "play some deep part in our sense of the overall direction of life: where do we go to, where do we come from? The sea, in particular, I think, has always represented the 'beyond'; what, if anything, lies beyond life." Water as a resonant image and symbol is consistently present in Swift's work, and Frumkes could be said to have identified, in his question, one of the keys to Swift's imagination. Swift is a poetic writer, with a gift for vivid image and metaphor. His settings and depictions of character are convincing both literally and figuratively—as credible physical realities, and as metaphoric constructions suggesting deeper, broader meanings. Water, for example, appears as an element of landscape and a symbol in his early fictions—in short stories like "Seraglio" and "Learning to Swim," where it suggests mystery and the paradoxical connectedness and alienation of human beings. In later works like *Waterland* and *Last Orders*, the sea emerges as an image of unknown eternity, the primal place of organicism and spirituality, of life and death.

To his poetic flare Swift also brings a strongly visceral sense of words. He has talked of his love for the English language as a "wonderfully concrete" tool for the writer, and his fiction leaves us with the indelible sense of physical worlds fully explored and appreciated. Not surprisingly, specificity is important to Swift's fiction. Setting is a major factor. Places — particularly in England, like London and the marshlands of East Anglia — achieve the presence of characters in his writing. In fact, setting works very closely with complex psychological characters helps to create Swift's richly detailed narratives and elucidate his themes.

His first novel, *The Sweet-Shop Owner*, introduces the characteristic Swiftian blend of setting and psychology combined to form both a concrete landscape and a poignant emotional geography. The novel focuses, as Swift's fictions often do, on a male narrator/ protagonist who is deeply attached to a specific place. Willy Chapman, like Jack Dodds in *Last Orders*, is inseparable from his store, which symbolically expresses both his love for children, and his need to escape life's hardships by selling dreams and ephemeral fantasies in the form of candy. Willy is the first of Swift's tormented older men, enmeshed in a family life that has deeply disappointed him. He is haunted by the ghost of his dead wife — the beautiful, remote, depressed seductress who regularly appears in Swift's fictions — and by his failure as a parent. The novel unfolds as a tale of loss and grief, with the lonely protagonist marooned in his own world by the end.

Shuttlecock picks up many of these themes and configurations, but casts them in the form of a psychological thriller, somewhat along the lines of John Fowles's *The Collector* or J. M. Coetzee's *Dusklands*. *Shuttlecock* also clearly reveals Swift's fascination with history, especially the history of the twentieth-century's two world wars. He has said that World War II in particular, and the admiration he continues to feel for his parents' generation, has nurtured his passionate interest in history. In *Shuttlecock*, the anti-heroic Swiftian protagonist, an alienated family man named Prentis, looks for a link between the past and present through the memoirs of his father, a war veteran. Here the father starts to emerge as the powerful, mythical figure he becomes in Swift's later works—a focus of enigmatic historical forces and the keeper of a cryptic legacy of misfortune and horror. Swift's preoccupation with death, and with the lingering presence of the dead in the world of the living, is also evident in this novel. Prentis works for the so-called "dead crimes" division of the police archives; obsolete crimes are his specialty. Here we see the fear of redundancy that stalks Swift's protagonists, and their sad sense of being left behind, somehow, by historical progress.

Learning to Swim encompasses a variety of themes and techniques. Plot is played down in these pieces for the most part, and each works as a kind of cameo—a "slice of life" or snapshot which captures a mood, an emotion, or an unexpected moment of crisis. The volume has an experimental feel to it; several of the stories isolate interesting aspects of Swift's technique that work together in an integrated way in his novels. His ability to vividly sketch a scene, to capture a character in a few sharp lines, is clearly shown here, for example. But the stories work best as psychological vignettes: brief studies of individuals caught in the ebb and flow of life, coping with the mundane world and trying to shoulder its sometimes overwhelming responsibilities. The most powerful piece is probably the title story, in which Swift focuses on one of the human configurations which deeply fascinates him: the nuclear family, consisting of woman, man, and child. The bonds of love and hate, dependency and resentment, which link the three people in the story are carefully explored through reminiscence and recollection. At the end, the child symbolically breaks away from the rigidity of the swimming lesson, and, defying both his parents, makes a bid for personal independence by striking out for the open sea.

This image of the boy trusting his body to the water and heading out to sea is also the concluding image of *Waterland*, where the family configuration — Swift's great theme of parents and children —

dominates a tragic pastoral tale of genetic and historical enmesh-ment. Many of the motifs and images of Swift's earlier work are fully articulated here, in what some critics still see as his finest novel. Swift's protagonist, the haunted, pain-wracked Tom Crick, a history teacher who has lost faith in the truth of his subject, unfolds a saga of Faulknerian dimensions in which, characteristically, the failure of human understanding in the face of history's complexity and the consolations of storytelling are woven together. In *Water-land*, Swift's strong sense of the limitations of knowledge and rati-ocination meets a deep longing for spiritual comfort which emerges clearly in his characters. The suicide of Tom's brother Dick at the end of the novel is portrayed as a mythical, semi-religious return to the primeval waters of both birth and death. His departure effaces the historical determinism that has both tempted and frustrated Tom. Dick's death is sacrificial; it suggests the possibility of salvation and the incipience, in the everyday world, of miracle.

The yearning for spiritual consolation reoccurs in Swift's fourth novel, *Out of this World*, in which modern society is shown as spiritually barren, materialistic, and frequently predatory. Like the Apollo astronauts landing on the moon in the novel's opening segment, the characters long to leave the world for some rarefied zone of serenity. Here Swift departs from the first-person point of view — for which he has stated a preference — and fragments the narrative, as he does again in *Last Orders*. The story of a troubled family haunted by the past — especially by the ancestral memory of World War II — *Out of this World* unfolds through a series of mon-ologues spoken by different characters. Swift's sense of history in this novel is extremely broad; his focus moves between the individ-ual and the wider arena of global events even more dramatically than in *Waterland*. Through Harry Beech, one of the novel's father-figures and a news photographer, Swift explores an idea that has become increasingly important in his fiction: the role, in the grand narrative of history, of the small and relatively obscure individual life. Harry's daughter Sophie, whose monologues are addressed to a psychiatrist, asks the loaded question: "How does it happen? How do our little lives get turned into these big shows? Even when all that's left of us is little pieces. How do they get made into public property?" (84). It is tempting to find the answer in a memorable phrase of Ray Johnson's, the main character in *Last Orders*: "It doesn't seem to help a man much, having been at the battle of El Alamain" (100).

In *Ever After*, Swift returns to the first-person point of view and immerses his narrative in the related ideas of death and rebirth. His protagonist, Bill Unwin, is a prematurely aged academic don who has survived a suicide attempt, and his story unfolds as a series of more or less tortured recollections. He is like Tom Crick taken to another level of despair, and the novel is a kind of psychological study of survivor's guilt. And yet, as so often in Swift's fictions, survival itself—in its stark factuality—has life-affirming symbolic connotations. Fascinated by death and the human journey towards death, Swift's work remains—ruefully and sometimes tenuously—wedded to life. The intertwining of death and life might perhaps be called Swift's over-arching theme. The dualities we encounter in his works—between body and mind, water and land, woman and man, for example—are shown to be deeply connected in ways which the narrative itself seeks out and reveals. In *Out of this World*, the psychiatrist Dr. Klein—who represents the "talking cure," psychoanalysis—declares: "It's telling that reconciles memory and forgetting" (74). Narrative itself can offer reconciliation and healing.

Swift never writes about death without also writing about life—its resilience, tenacity, and almost magical ability to reassert itself. The endlessness of storytelling is part of this stubborn magic. Images of resurrection abound in his work. In *Waterland*, for example, the eel illustrates the cyclicality of nature, asserting the principle of repetition against the bald cause-and-effect of history's forward march. Women and children often represent rebirth as well, although the lost or emotionally broken woman and the dead or damaged child also work as reminders of tragedy: the incomprehensible suffering of ordinary human life. Tom Crick, almost bereft of hope, nevertheless exhorts his pupils: "Children, be curious. Nothing is worse (I know it) than when curiosity stops. . . . Curiosity begets love. It weds us to the world. It's part of our perverse madcap love for this impossible planet we inhabit" (178).

Swift's novels strike a distinctly apocalyptic note. For many of his characters, the fear of the world ending is a springboard for spiritual exploration. It is usually through the central figure of the ruminative elderly man that the dread of apocalypse expresses itself at the personal level, as fear of death. In *Waterland, Ever After* and *Last Orders* — novels dominated by the dogged volubility of unhappy old men — the apparent finality of death can prove evanescent, for life begins again, in different forms and places, as time moves on and nature and history express themselves. Given these preoccupations, it is not surprising that Swift combines a strong sense of specificity with a mythic approach to narrative. His fictions create worlds that are both deeply particular and universal, characters who are both vividly individual and archetypal. Swift's sense of the contemporary is thus strongly informed by the past, and his engagement with twentieth-century history is permeated by his imaginative grasp of myth.

INFLUENCES

In its combination of the specific and the universal, as well as in many aspects of technique, Swift's work reveals the influence of Thomas Hardy, the late Victorian novelist whose fiction bridges the gap between the mid-nineteenth-century realist novel and the experimentation of early modernist fiction. Like Hardy's, Swift's fictions tend to be character-driven and philosophical, deeply concerned with both human psychology and the nature of our physical and spiritual lives. Looking to the ancient Greek dramatists, Hardy sought the grandeur of tragic emotion and experience in the quotidian life of his times. As he said in the General preface to the Wessex edition of his novels in 1912: "I considered that our magnificent heritage from the Greeks in dramatic literature found sufficient room for a large proportion of its action in an extent of their country not much larger than the half-dozen counties here reunited under the old name of Wessex, that the domestic emotions have throbbed in Wessex nooks with as much intensity as in the palaces of Europe, and that, anyhow, there was quite enough human nature in Wessex for one man's literary purpose." His characters, Hardy summarizes, are "beings in whose hearts and minds that which is apparently local should be really universal." The universal resonance of the human figure caught up with life and death in the local arena is Swift's thematic focus as well.

Hardy favored the omniscient narrative point-of-view and included in his work a rich sense of the particularity of England itself. Swift mostly avoids omniscience, preferring to strike the intimate note of the uninterrupted "I". But, like Hardy, he is a regionalist, at once faithfully portraying the English landscape and transforming it into a psychic and imaginative topography. Hardy was influenced by the ancient Greek tragedies of Aeschylus and Sophocles, and Swift, too, is immersed in some of the classic tragic patterns. He explores the suffering of families, the imperative of sexual desire, the warping of children by parents, and the drama of personal sacrifice. Incest also appears in his work, as a symbol of regression and misdirected entrepreneurial energy. Swift's emphasis on old men — their follies, regrets, and late-blooming greatness — recalls not only the Oedipus saga but Shakespeare's *King Lear.* The shock of old age, the existential horror of a desolate world, the betrayal of love, the failure of fathers, and the bitter grandeur — tattered but resolute — of the human soul are all aspects of Lear's tragedy which Swift draws on, particularly in *Waterland* and *Last Orders.*

Hardy's novels are strong on plot and mostly linear in their unfolding. Again like the Greeks, he builds ironic shifts of fortune and mysterious twists into his stories, so that the effort to find and understand the truth of a situation is part of what the narrative executes. Under the influence of the fractured narrative procedures of modernism, Swift eschews linearity for a temporal weave: different time-frames echo and intersect in his fiction — not to complicate plot, but to foreground perception itself as a problematic of narrative. In his concern with narrative frames and storytelling as a kind of layering — the building of a story vertically, rather than horizontally, as it were — Swift engages strongly with William Faulkner, a modernist deeply influenced himself by the Greek tragedians, Shakespeare, and Thomas Hardy.

Like Faulkner, Swift approaches the land itself as a character — a sort of wise, old man of great antiquity and resilience. His novels explore the face of the land, every gnarled wrinkle and cranny, insisting at once on its deep meaningfulness and the incommunicable nature of those meanings. The land is a repository of truth and dream, of history and legend for these writers. It is both expressive and frustratingly mute, powerfully eternal and fragile — liable to be lost, as the sea inundates the shore in *Waterland,* and as its weak custodians mismanage it in Faulkner's *Absolom, Absolom!* In the context of a landscape surrealistically imagined and hyper-embodied, Faulkner and Swift are both drawn to the epic tradition of Western literature, to self-divided heroes, archetypal journeys, family secrets, and dynastic sagas. The epic and the soap-opera, the tragedy and the melodrama, are some of the generic overlaps which both novelists favor. Apart from *The Sound and the Fury*, the influence of *As I Lay Dying*, Faulkner's 1930 novel, is particularly strong in Swift's later work. He has described *Last Orders* as a "homage" to *As I Lay Dying* and a reworking of an ancient narrative device: "The story about the pressure of the dead on the living, in the wake of death, is as old as Homer."

Although Swift's winning of the Booker Prize in 1996 was initially without controversy, the matter of *Last Orders*'s indebtedness to Faulkner later raised some conflict among critics. In a letter to the book review supplement of the newspaper *The Australian*, John Flow of the University of Queensland underlined some very close similarities in structure and subject-matter, including a monologue given to the dead person, a monologue consisting of numbered points, and a monologue made up of a single sentence. Swift was defended, in the *Guardian* newspaper and elsewhere, by colleagues like Philip Hobsbaum and Julian Barnes. The latter commented sharply: "When Brahms wrote his first symphony he was accused of having used a big theme from Beethoven's Ninth. His reply was that any fool could see that." Swift's frankness about his novel's references to *As I Lay Dying*, as well as the highly self-aware use of allusions in all his work, suggests a deliberate reworking of aspects of Faulkner's text.

Swift's use, in *Last Orders*, of the basic premise of Faulkner's novel — the tragi-comic journey of a bereaved family to bury its dead matriarch — signals not only his concern with Faulknerian themes, but with certain modernist techniques that Faulkner's work suggests. The disembodiment of voice, and the violent cracking open of the mundane to reveal the mythic are two examples of modernist approaches to narrative and experience which we find not only in Faulkner but in T. S. Eliot as well. *The Wasteland* (1922), Eliot's epoch-making poem of alienation and spiritual bankruptcy, echoes throughout Swift's oeuvre, particularly in *Waterland, Out of this World*, and *Last Orders*. The latter, with its spiritual searching, its dread of time, and its images of ashes and old men, also strongly recalls *The Four Quartets*. In some ways, Swift's deepest roots as a writer are in modernism, with its politically conservative and patriarchal impulses, although he questions these as well. Like some of his older contemporaries — Nadine Gordimer, for example — Swift might more accurately be termed a neo-modernist rather than a postmodernist.

In his senses of irony, humor — a sort of droll slapstick — and the grotesque, Swift reaches back not only to Faulkner and Hardy but also to Charles Dickens. One of the epigraphs to *Waterland* is a quotation from Dickens's classic swampland Bildungsroman, *Great Expectations*: "Ours was the marsh country." The legacy of Dickens manifests itself not just thematically in Swift's work — in his concern with childhood, sexuality, and the hero's passage from boy to man — but in a self-consciously historical way as well. Swift is well aware of the "great tradition" (as critic F. R. Leavis called it) of English literature within which he writes, and his fictions explore the strengths and limitations of that tradition partly through a deliberate process of imitation. *Waterland* is both a kind of copy of (a "homage" to) *Great Expectations*, and a parodic departure from it. Through this double perspective on the history of English literature, Swift signals his awareness of contemporary theories of the novel, and his sense that any twentieth-century writer must negotiate the novelists of the past — particularly, for him, the "classic" realists of the nineteenth-century, Charlotte Brönte, Charles Dickens, George Eliot, and Thomas Hardy.

This connection, both uneasy and admiring, to the "masters" of the genre associates Swift with other novelists of the later twentieth century, who have tried to work out what critic Harold Bloom calls "the anxiety of influence." Swift's fiction has especially strong resonances with Kazuo Ishiguro's, for both writers favor themes of isolation and eloquent bewilderment, in an England whose global position has changed. Both *Waterland* and *Last Orders* overlap with Ishiguro's *The Remains of the Day*. All three novels depict characters whose lives have been changed by the trauma of World War II, and who doubt their value as members of a postwar British society in which the power of empire has dwindled and the country's historical mission is profoundly unclear. The Canadian Michael Ondaatje's novel *The English Patient* also travels this same thematic terrain. Unlike, say, Angela Carter, Salman Rushdie or Jeanette Winterson, Swift, Ishiguro, and Ondaatje eschew fabulism, fantasy and science-fiction in their portrayals of postcolonial England. The idiosyncratic magic realism that is becoming a vernacular of the contemporary British novel is replaced in their work by an almost old-fashioned sense of decorum, as if each novelist is testing the limits of the language and the art-form in its traditional uses. In relation to certain of his contemporaries, then, Swift shares, but also departs from, many of the preoccupations of British postmodernism.

To the inexorability of Hardy's tragic vision, Swift brings a late twentieth-century self-consciousness about storytelling. Like Ishiguro, Winterson, and Barnes, he explores the interchange between reader and text in a post-realist age where traditional narrative structures and sub-genres (like the Bildungsroman) have been questioned. In the strand of narrative experimentation and metafictional awareness which runs through Swift's work, we see his engagement not only with his peers (he has interviewed both Ishiguro and Caryl Phillips) but also with the generation of British writers who emerged just after World War II. Specifically, Swift's work echoes that of John Fowles (especially *The French Lieutenant's Woman* [1969]) in its preoccupation with the relationship between nineteenth- and twentieth-century England, and the art of novel-writing as it was practiced then and is practiced now.

Like Fowles, who is himself deeply influenced by Hardy, Swift explores the function of fiction in the skeptical contemporary world. On the whole, he tends to affirm its on-going value — as an almost magical source of wisdom and comfort for human beings. Both novelists articulate this belief through a somewhat idealistic portrayal of women. Like Sarah Woodruff in *The French Lieutenant's Woman*, Mary Crick and Amy Dodds are semi-mythic figures of femininity and desire. They recall Hardy's Well-Beloved and her various incarnations, in his other novels, as Eustacia Vye, Bathsheba Everdene, Tess Derbyfield, and Sue Bridehead. Like Hardy and Fowles, Swift depicts women ambiguously — as ideals, but also as destructive figures. They are at once redemptive and deceitful, like the fateful, elusive temptresses of certain Victorian misogynist works — in some of Zola's fictions, for examples, or Wilde's.

In this regard, Swift's work contains various echoes of Fowles's great novel of mid-twentieth-century male angst, *The Magus* (1966; 1978). Here, the existential and sexual crisis of an ordinary Englishman is woven together with recent historical events and played out in a context both concrete and mythical. On a Greek island in the 1950s, various atrocious events of World War II are enacted heuristically for the education of a callow man. Although Swift avoids the fantastic elements of Fowles's novel, the motifs of intergenerational conflict, sexual misadventure, emotional pain, the impinging of history on the individual, and spiritual longing all resonate in different parts of his oeuvre.

I earlier described Swift as poetic in his approach to novel writing, and I have mentioned the resonances of T. S. Eliot in his work. To read Swift's fiction is to find many rich echoes, not only of other novelists and playwrights, but of poets as well. In his concern with death, time, and the human struggle for spiritual consolation, Swift recalls Alfred Tennyson, whose poems about loss — particularly "In Memoriam" and "Crossing the Bar" — strike the same mixed note of bereaved hope. There is something of the severe honesty of Robert Frost in Swift's clear-eyed examination of life's challenges, and Frost's tone of mournfully circumspect anger sounds at times in Swift's prose. In his emphasis on the relationship between body and soul, the physical world and the evanescent realm of the spirit, Swift's writing shows a mystical touch reminiscent of Gerard Manley Hopkins. Swift's powerful, loving sense of nature, and the exhilarated wonder that can break through the sadness and incomprehension of his characters recall the potent mixture of joy and grief in Hopkins's poems. There are other poetic echoes too, both ancient and modern—from Old English poetry to Philip Larkin and Ted Hughes. Swift's modernity, then, is based on and emerges from an immersion in the literary traditions of the West and of the English language.

2

The Novel

PLOT AND CHARACTER

In Swift's novels, a simple plot usually provides the opportunity for a profound study of character, and a complex journey into the human psyche. As a writer deeply interested in the mind and its relationship to the heart, Swift uses plot as a point of departure for exploring the personalities and relationships of his vivid individuals. We could say that not very much actually happens in Swift's novels and stories. The plot of *Waterland*, for example, is barely concrete at all. It takes the form of an extended meditation. After the confinement of his wife Mary to a hospital for the mentally ill, the narrator Tom Crick recalls their life, twining together his own memories with his knowledge of the history of East Anglia to create a memoir both private and public, personal and documentary. The element of meditation and stasis in *Waterland* recurs in Swift's other fictions: in the story "Learning to Swim," for example, plot as a sequence of events is replaced by an occasion, the single event of a father giving his son a swimming lesson, and the "action" of the story consists mostly of the boy's mother's meditation about her marriage and her child. The subtlety of Swift's technique as a novelist comes partly from the skill with which he represents thought and feeling as a kind of action, weaving character over a skeleton of plot which seems fragile, but which suits his purposes entirely.

The plot of *Last Orders* is typically straightforward. After the death of one of their friends, a group of working-class Londoners travels by car to Margate, a seaside town, to scatter his ashes as he requested, into the sea. There is a good deal of movement involved in the plot of *Last Orders*, though, for it describes a physical journey, and one of the main themes explored in the novel is motion itself. Swift's characters tend to be searchers: they look for truth and understanding in a world that baffles them. Most often, they search internally. Men like Tom Crick are emotional and intellectual explorers, examining terrain both actual (the marshlands of Essex) and imaginatively transformed. In fact, fear of motion and a mistrust of travel often mark Swift's people. But in *Last Orders*, Swift literalizes the idea of seeking through his use of the ancient narrative device of the journey. The four men, compelled by a common errand, travel together across a small part of England, making discoveries about themselves, each other, their world, time and history.

At the center of the journey from London to Margate is the huge and generous butcher, Jack Arthur Dodds. Jack's position at the core of the plot is not a simple one, however, as his is the death that initiates the journey. Like the character of Addy, the dead mother in Faulkner's *As I Lay Dying*, the most important character in *Last Orders* is missing—although powerfully present as well, in the memories of the other characters. Also like Addy, Jack has the opportunity to address the reader from beyond death, as it were, for he has a brief narrative section of his own near the novel's end. The ontological ambiguity of Jack Dodds—part fact, part fiction; there and not there—becomes a way for Swift to question both the para-meters of the individual life, and the meshing of that life with other lives and with wider, less tangible time-frames. Absurd as it sounds, "Where has Jack gone?" is a question the novel invites us to ask, and thus to pursue our own meditation on the relations, physical and metaphysical, between life and death.

In a sense, Jack Dodds, even though he is dead at the story's start, is not dead at all. His great physique and ego, his facility with meat, and his strengths and weaknesses continue to grip the imagination of the people who knew him. Seen in the light of such powerful memories, the journey to scatter Jack's ashes is both an acknowledgement of his passing and a recognition that he will never pass. Jack Dodds, Family Butcher, remains, in a way, the beating heart of the small community depicted in *Last Orders*. Dead on arrival in terms of the novel's plot, he remains vividly alive at its core, just as his native Smithfield, the meat-packing district of London, endures as the city's bleeding but resilient heart.

Last Orders begins, just after Jack's funeral, in Bermondsey, a working-class area of London. It opens in a pub called The Coach and Horses, where the five men have gathered regularly over many years. Here we meet the group who have undertaken to carry out the "last orders" of their old friend: Ray Johnson, Vince Dodds, Vic Tucker, and Lenny Tate. We meet them through their voices. The novel is structured as a series of monologues, most of them spoken by the four friends, although Jack himself has one, his daughter-in-law Mandy has one, and his widow Amy (a crucial character in the novel) has six. *Last Orders* is a fine example of "ensemble playing" in narrative form, for the voices meld and separate, just as the personalities of the characters unfold discretely and collectively.

Ray Johnson, an insurance clerk, is nevertheless the most prominent of the men. Jack's best friend and war buddy, Ray is effectively the novel's protagonist and the closest it gets to a single organizing consciousness. Ray narrates most of the sections, which are headed with the names of each speaker, and he also narrates those sections named for the places through which the men travel. It is Ray's perspective which dominates, and Ray himself acquires rich symbolic meaning as the novel proceeds. Ray is a betting man, sharp as his name, with a remarkable eye for the winner in any horse race. Jack long ago nicknamed him "Lucky," and he slowly emerges as a kind of spiritual counterpart to the blunt, fleshy Dodds. Ray becomes the novel's symbol of hope: "a little ray of sunshine . . . a little ray of hope," as Amy describes him (284). Although tiny, he is the strongest of all the men. He carries most of the emotional burden of Jack's death and, because he comes to stand for the future as well as the past, he bears the weight of the story by narrating most of it.

The other three men reveal themselves to us as the journey begins. On the way out of busy London, we hear from Vince Dodds, Jack's adopted son, who, at forty, is the youngest of the group. Vince is a rebel, having rejected the Dodds family tradition by refusing to enter the meat trade. A used-car dealer and the most materially successful of the men, Vince has chosen the car for the occasion: a royal blue Mercedes with cream seats. "It's a 380 S-Class, that's what it is," Vince gloats, "V8, automatic. It's six years old but it could do a hundred and thirty without a wobble" (23). A large number of the novel's sections are narrated by Vince, whose complex love/hate relationship with Jack reinforces the powerful theme of family relationships and, in particular, the connection between fathers and sons. This connection is reiterated in the dignified, restrained Vic Tucker, the undertaker who arranged Jack's funeral and cremation. Vic's two sons have followed family tradition, entering their father's business and ensuring an unbroken line of commercial succession. Partly for this reason, Vic's family life is remarkably peaceful. Rather like Jack, Vic has struggled with a profession which typecasts him as negative and sinister; but he has achieved serenity in what the novel presents as the undertaker's nurturing role. Through Vic, Swift expresses the inevitability and unexpected comfort of death, as well as its ability to equalize all people in a common mortality.

Vic also brings into the novel—first into the pub and then into the car—what's left of Jack in the story's narrative present: his ashes, in "a plastic container. It looks like a large instant coffee jar," muses Ray, "it's got the same kind of screw-on cap. But it's not glass, it's a bronzy-coloured, faintly shiny plastic" (3). As the journey proceeds, the jar of ashes becomes a very ambiguous object, and the men squabble repeatedly over who will hold and carry it, and how it should be carried. The jar and its contents implicitly pose philosophical questions about the body, which is always an object of intense fascination in Swift's work. Without his conspicuous flesh, having acquired a "body" of ash, Jack is unaccountably changed. Through the complicated materiality of his remains, the novel emphasizes the mysterious, almost magical nature of flesh while further exploring the interplay of body and spirit, both in the individual and the world at large. The unobtrusive jar becomes, moreover, an interesting counterpart to the flashy automobile. Both are containers, vehicles, for the novel's larger questions about life's purpose—the destination of the human journey—and the uncertainty of England's future in the twenty-first century.

The last of the group of friends is Lenny Tate, a fruit-and-vegetable-dealer by trade and the poorest, angriest of the men. Lenny is, as Ray often says, "a stirrer," drawing to the surface the hidden tensions among the friends, stirring up the remnants of the past out of which the story is woven. Lenny, a foil for the reconciliatory Vic, imports visceral action into the plot. His belligerence sparks the novel's most violent incident—the fist-fight between himself and Vince at Wick's Farm in Kent, popularly called "the Garden of England" (106). Furthermore, Lenny's resentment against

Vince for having abandoned his pregnant daughter years before emphasizes the connection in the novel between fathers and daughters. Ray, Vince, Lenny, and Jack have all had troubled relationships with their only daughters, and these conflicts raise the important thematic issues of inheritance, reproduction, and sexuality. "Daughters," snorts Lenny, like a modern King Lear, "Who'd have 'em?" (47).

The women characters are very important in *Last Orders*, even though none are included on the trip to Margate, which is an exclusively male undertaking. The business of scattering Jack's ashes becomes, as Ray speculates, "a blokes' job" (21), but a "job" profoundly informed by the motives and desires of the absent women. These comprise Amy Dodds, Jack's widow; Mandy Dodds, Vince's wife; Sally, Kath, and Susie, the daughters respectively of Lenny, Vince, and Ray; and June, Jack and Amy's mentally handicapped daughter, who never appears or speaks in the novel. In addition, Vic's wife Pam, Lenny's wife Joan, Ray's ex-wife Carol, and her sister Daisy are briefly mentioned. Although all these women, even June, are closely linked through family ties to the novel's male characters, they form a spectral group of their own, which haunts and complicates the bluff masculinity of the group of men.

The major woman character — and the closest the novel gets to a heroine — is Amy, who refuses to be involved in the disposal of Jack's remains, but who accompanies the men imaginatively and in spirit. Most of her monologues cluster in the last quarter of the novel. As the travelers draw closer to their destination, Amy imagines what they are doing. As the story draws to its end and the final letting go of Jack, Amy tells the story of their early days — their brief courtship and marriage, the birth of June, and the adoption of Vince during World War II. The crucial idea which Amy brings to the story is that of the circularity of time. Through Amy's narratives, the effective beginning of the story — what preceded and gave rise to the journey to Margate — unfolds concurrently with its ending; cause and effect are compelled into a single frame of simultaneous narration and remembrance, and *Last Orders* (despite the finality of its title) enacts a circular motion.

The circle is a traditional symbol of completion and perfection, of beginnings and endings rolled into one — or, to express it differently, of the impossibility of precisely identifying the beginning and the end. Swift draws on all these implications in *Last Orders*. In deploying the circle as an implied structural device, he harks back to one of the modernist writers whose influence upon his work is marked: Virginia Woolf. Both *Mrs. Dalloway* and *To the Lighthouse* are novels about journeying which take as their conceptual foundation the primal journey of the human being from life into death. *To the Lighthouse* in particular, with its strong sense of horizontal motion broken by the soaring verticals of structures like the lighthouse, echoes in Swift's fascination with grief, movement, and the symbolic replacement of lost human beings with the compensatory strategies of representation. Like Lily Briscoe completing her painting just as Mr. Ramsay and his children reach the lighthouse symbolizing the dead Mrs. Ramsay, Amy completes the story of Jack as his ashes — a substitute for the man himself — are delivered to the sea by those who loved him.

This idea of circularity and completion through spiritual questing, and the expression of love through art, are themes of modernist writing which Swift reworks in the late twentieth century. Furthermore, the circular motion described in *Last Orders* directly recalls T. S. Eliot's famous lines — implying a fundamentally religious attitude towards time — from *Four Quartets*: "In my end is my beginning." Among other things, the circle is the shape of spiritual comfort, of return and renewal, for Woolf, Eliot, and Swift.

As a novelist, Swift is also interested in the circle as a sign of the indeterminacy of narrative itself, and of its ambiguous double, history. In *Waterland*, Tom Crick, a history teacher, wrestles with the difficulties of narration, of cause and effect, and the problem of determining beginnings and ends. In *Last Orders*, the apparent finality of death spurs a questioning of the logic of human life — a logic which proves as ambiguous as death itself, for Jack endures despite his departure, and the unaware June is effectively dead despite her living on in an institution. Thus the linear model for understanding life and the human journey through time works concurrently with the circular model, whereby the passage of time is collapsed in a form which reconciles the poles of the journey by blurring them together. In Swift's work, the emblem for this ambiguous circularity of time, life, and death is the woman. The female body is a deeply symbolic place in his fictions: the point both of origins and conclusions, beginnings and endings, life and death.

Swift's heroines are, in a sense, goddesses. They suggest an archetypal femininity: "woman" as a kind of eternal principle. As in *Waterland*, the female characters in *Last Orders* blend impressionistically into one: a single force of enigmatic womanhood, working variously as perennial object of male desire, as mother, as the bearer of universal human experience, and as the vessel of harsh wisdom. Ray expresses the primordial interconnectedness of the women when he watches his daughter Susie drying her hair: "I can't deny it, she's better-looking than Carol ever was, even Carol at her age. It's a kind of disrespect and unfairness to Carol to think it but that don't matter because she's a part of Carol, there's a part of Carol in her" (51). Amy, like Mary Crick in *Waterland*, is a mythic figure. She is a mixture of Eve, both before and after the Fall, and the Virgin Mary. She is the siren who entrances Jack, Ray, and Lenny; the mother who sacrifices her marriage out of loyalty to her daughter; and the crone who abandons her husband's remains and effectively disobeys his last orders. Like a pagan deity, Amy is both the life-giver and the death-dealer of the novel. She makes love with both Jack and Ray; she gives birth, but her only offspring is June, whose handicap makes her one of the "living dead." Amy is a figure of hope in its earthy, fleshy incarnation as sex and romantic passion; yet she stands also for the death that is inevitably a part of nature.

Along with her biblical connotations, Amy strongly recalls Ceres, the classical goddess of the harvest, especially in the monologue describing her first meeting with Jack during a pre-war summer of hop-picking at Wick's Farm. Like Ceres, Amy brings the consolations of repetition. She stands for the repetitiveness of natural cycles and the endless cyclicality of time itself. Her very body suggests her symbolic roles. Recalling when she and Jack prepared beans for cooking in the hop fields, Amy describes how she "jammed the colander between [her] thighs" and invited Jack to throw the stringed beans into it: " 'See if we can't fill it' " (237). The round colander represents her own round, inner space, her uterus: "And there was that feeling inside me, between me, like a bowl" (237). Compelled by (what Swift depicts as) the woman's primal desire to be filled, Amy's body speaks of instinct and a kind of irrational knowledge that counters logic and rationality in the novel, and borders on the mysterious spiritual knowledge explored in the second half of *Last Orders*.

The novel's other women characters are, in a sense, all versions of Amy Dodds. In Swift's fiction, the archetypal nature of women turns them all into variations on the same theme — of desire and seduction, mystery, maternity, and death. Like Carol and Susie, Mandy is a younger version of her mother-in-law, replacing Amy (as well as Sally Tate) in Vince's oedipal drama. Both Amy and Mandy make love in Ray's camper, which becomes, in Vince's words, a "passion wagon" (102) for two generations of lovers. Through this echoing of older and younger women — the layering of symbolic "mothers" and "daughters" — the circularity for which women stand in Swift's work is literally embodied. It is, moreover, linked to his overarching theme of time and history through inter-generational relationships. As the generations succeed, rebel against, and reiterate each other, the linearity of time is both stressed and questioned in the novel, and the idea of the journey is prominently emphasized.

THE JOURNEY

The simple plot of *Last Orders* is structured through the rich literary device of the journey. Here Swift draws on Western literature's venerable tradition of narratives shaped by the idea of journeying, from Homer's *Odyssey* to Ishiguro's *The Remains of the Day*. Strategically, the journey facilitates the unfolding of plot by anchoring it in place and offering different geographical sites for dramatic action. The journey is also a flexible yet clear way for a writer to foreground themes of growth and change, to show human psychology in process, and to problematize the conventional narrative stages of beginning, middle, and end. In these ways, the device of the journey invites an investigation not just of the content of stories, but of the very processes of storytelling. Narrative itself can be seen as a journey, a movable feast of fiction and fact, invention and documentary. In *Last Orders*, Swift uses the journey to further explore the complexities of narrative — particularly the interplay between story, history, and memory — which so fascinated him in his earlier novels.

Journeys are crucial to the ancient myths that have shaped cultures throughout time. In the Western tradition alone, questing heroes from Ulysses and Jason to Beowulf, Arthur's knights, Gulliver, and David Copperfield trace the deep parallels between physical travel and inner searching. Their stories shape the journey as variously a rite of passage, a moral and spiritual ordeal, and a search for knowledge or enlightenment. In twentieth-century quest narratives, such as Joseph Conrad's *Heart of Darkness* and James Joyce's *Ulysses*, the wandering or travelling hero searches not only to comprehend his own soul and mind, but also to understand the destiny of his race or country. In *Heart of Darkness*, Marlow's search for the elusive Kurtz in the jungles of the Belgian Congo is not only a psychological journey into the enigmatic human heart, but an inquiry into modern history, as Conrad questions the right of the European powers to colonize Africa.

In *Ulysses*, too, Joyce uses the journey device to explore questions of Irish national identity, bringing a specifically political inflection to the mythic import of the quest. Implying as it does notions of progress and regression, the journey functions pragmatically as a tool for historical analysis, inviting the kind of political questioning undertaken by Ishiguro in *Remains*, by Conrad in *Heart*, or by E. M. Forster in *A Passage to India*, for example. In *Last Orders*, Swift (like Ishiguro) builds on the social concerns of the modernist quest narrative to ask difficult questions about England's historical destination in the aftermath of Empire.

Swift works closely in *Last Orders* with many different resonances of the journey. He combines the powerful sense of archetypal humanity discovered in mythic journeys with the historically-specific political emphasis found in later revisions of the device. Although he avoids focusing on a single protagonist exclusively, Swift echoes the *Odyssey* in both its Homeric and Joycean forms, moving lucidly between the trials of the individual quester(s) and the larger, social/philosophical implications of the quest. He also gives the journey a precisely English emphasis by drawing on two of the earliest quest narratives in the language, the Old English poems *The Wanderer* and *The Seafarer*, which describe poignantly the psychic and physical effects of a journey by land and by sea respectively. Longing, rootlessness, the haunting properties of space itself, and the exhilaration of freedom are among the moods of these ancient poems reworked vividly for contemporary readers in *Last Orders*.

To these echoes of the beginnings of English literature, Swift adds those of a period very important to his work: the nineteenth century. Swift's fiction is deeply involved with the tradition of English realism that flowered at that time, in the novels of Charlotte Brönte, George Eliot, Thomas Hardy, and Charles Dickens. From Dickens, Swift takes the premises of the English Bildungsroman or novel of education: the shaping idea of an individual's development from youth to maturity—an idea that harks back to very early English novels, like John Bunyan's *The Pilgrim's Progress*, and forward to brilliant riffs on the notion of personal growth, like Joyce's *A Portrait of the Artist as a Young Man*. Primarily, though, Swift draws on the idea of the religious journey, and *Last Orders* deliberately echoes that English saga of pilgrimage, Chaucer's *The Canterbury Tales*. The four men undertake their journey in April, when spring brings both death and life—the death of the old and the birth of the new. Shaken by loss, the friends implicitly seek new growth and life, just as Chaucer's pilgrims long to find regeneration for their souls by journeying to the tomb of St. Thomas Becket, in Canterbury Cathedral: "And specially from every shires end/Of Engelond to Caunterbury they wende/The hooly blisful martir for to seke/That hem hath holpen whan that they were seeke."

In Swift's novel, the impromptu visit to the Cathedral confirms the men's errand as a spiritual quest—for revelation, truth, and community—in the face of the riddles of time and death. In terms of plot, the visit to the Cathedral is a climax of sorts, for it follows the visit to the war memorial at Chatham and the fistfight at Wick's Farm. In the latter two episodes, the men confront loss in both its national and deeply personal forms. At the naval memorial, the bald fact of death meets them in the listed names of the war dead. Mortality shocks the travelers here, for the dead fighters are practically forgotten. The obelisk of the memorial recalls the effectively anonymous tombs of the ancient Egyptians, and the inscription over the gates rings ironically for the four worn-out survivors of Britain's twentieth-century conflicts: "All These Were Honoured In Their Generations And Were The Glory Of Their Times" (129).

At Wick's Farm, where Vince—gripped by uncharacteristic emotion—scatters some of Jack's ashes, the men re-experience the intense grief of their friend's death in the context of other defeats: the loss of love, family life, and emotional connection. Wick's Farm, the place where Jack and Amy met and where June was conceived, is a scene of primal loss for Vince. On subsequent stops at the Farm, during day trips to the beach with his adoptive parents and Lenny's daughter, Sally, Vince sensed that the very place of his parents' happiness was also the place of their losing it, for the brief, passionate love of Amy and Jack did not survive accidental pregnancy, marriage, and the birth of an unwanted child. Given these echoes, the fight between Lenny and Vince in "the Garden of England" becomes mythic and biblical: a version of the aftermath of humanity's fall from grace in the garden of Eden—a fall effected through curiosity and sexuality in a gloriously pastoral setting. In a way, Lenny and Vince become the warring brothers, Cain and Abel, and the visit to the Cathedral is Swift's way of bringing hope, redemption, and forgiveness to the universal human struggle not only with death, grief, anger, and loss, but also with desire and the seductiveness of knowledge.

As Lenny comments, stopping at the Cathedral gives the travelers a salutary "dose of holiness" after dissension (195). It reunites them under the auspices of faith after their encounters with difficult knowledge—the knowledge of both England's historical past and that of their own small community of Bermondsey. At Chatham, the weight of history—the incomprehensibility of war and national sacrifice—bears down on the fragile, mortal human being. The generations are divided by battles which seem irrelevant now, and even the act of remembering—memorializing—becomes suspect. Looking at the names, Vince sums up the disillusion of his generation and the failure of empathy between England's "fathers" and "sons": "Old buggers" (130). Beside the sad, doubtful grandeur of the memorial, the plastic jar containing Jack's ashes appears doubly absurd and meaningless. In *Last Orders*, Swift asks the same profound question about history as he asked in *Waterland*: what is the relation between the individual human life and the broader life of the race, or the species?

At Wick's Farm, Vince's desperate desire to scatter some of Jack in a paradisal place where love once flowered asserts the human need to find meaning in each single death, and to shore up memory as our only access to immortality. But conflict and rage, endemic to human affairs, erupt at every level, even the most intimate. Lenny, burdened by his old resentment of Vince, is enraged at the latter's assumption of control of the jar: "Toe-rag,'" says Lenny, "toe-rag. He aint got no prior claim" (145). The fight is based on wounded pride, grief, and the desire for revenge. These primeval impulses are the consequences of humanity's lost innocence, and faith (Swift implies) is a deeply necessary response to them. Although Canterbury Cathedral is itself replete with history—"What's the lick and spit of a human life against fourteen centuries?" asks Ray (201)—and, at least at the structural level, meets fragile mortality with a grandeur even greater than that of the war memorial, its sacred character lends it a different, more comforting, symbolic meaning. Gazing up at the wheeling Gothic columns, Ray reads their spiritual import: "The pillars go up and up, then they fan out like they're not pillars any more, they've let go of their own weight and it's not stone any more, it's not material. It's like wings up there arching

and reaching. . . . The next world" (207). As a sacred memorial, the
Cathedral is a kind of gateway to another world, a spiritual portal,
unlike the melancholy secularity of the memorial at Chatham.

At Canterbury Cathedral, the men are symbolically cleansed
before continuing their journey to the sea. The weightlessness of
the architecture speaks of unburdening and redemption: the miraculous translation, beyond death, of matter into spirit. The Cathedral
is a place of renewal and spiritual hope, for even though Ray finds
the "next world" imaginatively unreachable, he receives an intimation of it. Human frailty is here accepted, incorporated, and prom-
ised transformation. Even Edward Plantagenet, the notorious Black
Prince, resides here in death, like any old flawed "geezer" in need
of God's grace. In the context of the venerable church — a memorial
both to history and faith — the stone tomb of Edward, like Jack's
plastic jar, becomes a sign of bodily metamorphosis, and the last
trace of the soul's passage beyond flesh and blood.

Like Chaucer, Swift uses the idea of a pilgrimage to make the
journey a collective effort, a problematic of human relationships, as
well as a search for understanding and, crucially, for the grace of
God. The importance of the miraculous to Swift's vision of modern
life can hardly be overstated. His fiction is preoccupied with the
limits of rationality — the failures of human knowledge — and the
mysterious possibilities of intuition and spiritual insight. Rationality
and faith debate with each other as alternate ways of knowing in
Swift's work. Faith is suggested throughout *Last Orders* by the weird
luck of "Lucky" Johnson; its deep link to hope, even in the face of
disillusion, is implied in the search for love in which every character
is privately engaged. The presence of God, like the presence of Jack
Dodds, becomes a moot point in the novel. Intimations of grace
signal the pressures placed, in Swift's fictions, upon human systems
of knowledge by faith, revelation, and miracle. If the four friends'
journey becomes, as the pilgrimage does in *The Canterbury Tales*,

a tragi-comic chronicle of human strengths and failings, the Cathedral offers a place of absolution, releasing into the novel the possibility of forgiveness and reconciliation. In the light of the strong references in *Last Orders* to *The Canterbury Tales*, we can see how the stages of the journey marked by the pilgrims' progress become spiritual stations, recalling ultimately the stations of Christ's cross, and the human longing for salvation, peace, and meaningful sacrifice.

Through these multiple resonances, a palimpsestic layering of ancient and modern literary voices, Swift broadens the range of *Last Orders* in a highly metafictional way. He brings a myriad of other fictional journeys to bear on this, the one most lately ordered, and invites us to consider the entire history of English literature as itself a kind of journey. When the transformed body of Jack Dodds finally reaches the limit of the land and his ashes are taken by the wind, the symphony of intertexts in the novel requires the reader to ask, "Where is English literature itself headed, in the twenty-first century?" In posing this question, Swift takes his place among the major British novelists of the post-1945 era. Like his older contemporaries John Fowles and Iris Murdoch, as well as his younger ones, Salman Rushdie, Ishiguro, and Jeanette Winterson, Swift's concern with the past and future of modern England is both historical and literary. As England's power dwindles in the wake of imperialism, these writers explore the heritage of English literature as a shifting legacy, liable to lose or change its meanings as the postcolonial world emerges. Like Jack Dodds himself, English literature (as well as English history and even the English language) is on an adventure, facing translation, hovering on the brink of an unrealized but intimated "next world."

I have said that the journey to scatter Jack's ashes is a male enterprise in the novel. The four men travel from the city to the coast, from land to sea, in a movement which suggests expansiveness and a kind of liberation. At the brink of the land—and here *Last Orders* once again echoes *The Remains of the Day*—the ocean offers both oblivion and freedom: the freedom of conversion into another element; the tracklessness of water. This outward trajectory of the male journey to the shore is counterpointed in the novel by the inward trajectory of the journeys undertaken by the women. Although Susie, a member of the hyper-mobile younger generation, takes off for Australia, the other two female travelers, Mandy and Amy, pursue landlocked journeys, towards home rather than away from it.

Mandy has only one monologue in the novel. She describes how she ran away from her home in Blackburn, Lancashire, only to find herself in another home, the Dodds', in Bermondsey: "So Mandy Black, or Judy Battersby as she was travelling as, arrived in London in a meat lorry and got carted away again in a butcher's van, without so much as a peep at Leicester Square" (156). Mandy's brief experience of being on the road suggests a potential quest which never took place: "That was my adventure, my big adventure, though it hardly lasted twelve hours" (157). Hers is the truncated or aborted story of the female explorer, which culminates in Mandy's assumption of the traditional feminine roles of wife, mother, and homemaker. The tedium of domesticity—the historylessness of the hearth—is a strong preoccupation of Swift's. His emphasis on romance and sexual passion in heterosexual relationships articulates in another way the theme of time in his work. Swift's men and women usually experience their greatest fulfillment as lovers, rather than as husbands and wives. The ardent love affair which dwindles quickly into a featureless marriage is a recurring motif in his fiction. Such marriages, and the troubled parenthood which often accompanies them, are forms of living death for Swift, confirmations of the perversity and illogicality of time and life. Through the transforming of passionate mistresses into disillusioned wives, Swift brings to his vision of modernity a critique of marriage and a complex investigation of constraining gender roles.

Amy refuses to go to Margate partly because of her regularly-scheduled visit to June in the institution. She keeps the fires of home burning by restricting her journeying to the bus that runs from the city to the hospital: "This is where I belong, number 44. . . . As if as long as there's a number 44 going from London Bridge to Mitcham Cricketers the world won't fall apart, London Bridge won't fall down" (230). Through Amy's repetitive and circum-scribed movement—the movement of a mother to and from her child—Swift emphasizes the effect of placement and location in human life; he engages the idea of home, and the related spatial question of the relationship between margin and center, the para-meters and the core. Drawing a contrast between the trajectories of the male and female travelers in the novel, Swift explores what constitutes a home, what it means to move around in the world, and how gender functions as a determinant of freedom.

THE BODY

The human body provides a strong and consistent image pattern in *Last Orders*, anchoring the text's main thematic concerns. The novel is predicated upon the body of Jack Dodds—its propensities during life and its transformations in death. It is Jack's body that unites the group of travelers in a common purpose, that continues to hold the imagination of those around him, and that finally must be relinquished in the novel's closing moments. Swift is deeply interested in the body: its extraordinary capacities, how it changes over time, the compelling quality of the flesh itself, and how its energies and impulses motivate us. One of the epistemological questions *Last Orders* puzzles over is the metamorphosis of the flesh in death. What *are* Jack's ashes, existentially speaking? Are they simply equivalent to the coffee which Vince buys in Rochester and carries, together with the urn, in a plastic shopping bag? How do Jack's ashes relate to the man he was? How should they be treated and honored? And, of course, the crucial question: where has Jack gone? How do human beings engage with the notion of "the next world"? With these latter questions, as I have suggested, the line between body and spirit is blurred, and *Last Orders* takes on its subtly religious tone.

Jack Dodds's body, the basis for exploring these issues, becomes effectively inseparable from his occupation as a butcher. A fleshy man, Jack manages and trades in the flesh of animals. In this, he is both contrasted to and paralleled with the undertaker Vic Tucker, who manages and disposes of the flesh of human beings. With their establishments located near each other in Bermondsey, Jack had one or two opportunities to help Vic out in emergency situations. Vic's recollection of Jack's alacrity with dead people sets up similarities in the novel between human and animal flesh, and between the slaughter of animals and the sacrifices made by human beings. Requesting help with a corpse one hot and busy day, Vic asked, " 'You sure about this?' " and Jack replied, " 'I've seen bodies.' . . . 'Yes, but not women,' " says Vic. "But [Jack] didn't turn a hair, didn't bat an eyelid, as if a seventy-four-year-old woman who's died crossing the road wasn't any different from a joint of beef" (85). Talking with Ray in the hospital just before he dies, Jack comments on the power of chance in life: "No telling is there?" Then he says, "Lambs to the slaughter, eh Lucky" (152).

The inevitability of death, along with its leveling power across nature's entire spectrum, brings the human and the animal poignantly close. In a sense, all human life becomes sacrificial. Jack Dodds, "Master butcher" (28), is in his turn masterfully butchered — by illness, the surgeon's knife, and fire, before being given over to the wind and the sea. Through such vivid physical imagery, Swift evokes the body as elemental—a kind of earth, ready to take its place among the other elements—and death becomes a return to primal organic matrix. Throwing the last handful of Jack into the water at Margate, Ray ends the novel with the words: "and the ash that I carried in my hands, which was the Jack who once walked around, is carried away by the wind, is whirled away by the wind till the ash becomes wind and the wind becomes Jack what we're made of" (295).

What distinguishes the human from the animal body, though, is summed up in the novel's first epigraph, taken from Sir Thomas Browne's 1658 treatise on death and spirituality, *Urn Burial*: "But man is a Noble Animal, splendid in ashes, and pompous in the grave." In its self-consciousness, the human animal aspires to nobility; it seeks to comprehend death in a deeper way, through ritual and ceremony, and to find splendor even in remains. Humans bring a spiritual awareness to the brute factuality of death—although the danger here, the quotation implies, is arrogance and too great a sense of self-importance. From the point of view suggested by the epigraph, Vic the undertaker may be seen as a kind of priest of the body, and Jack the butcher as a kind of doctor. Significantly, medicine was the career that Jack would have chosen for himself, had he not been bound by family tradition.

The common denominator of organic life is flesh. But, as Browne suggests, the human being is more complex than the animal; the human body is more mysterious and unpredictable, because caught up inevitably with intelligence, emotion, and spirit. The pungency of the epigraph is especially marked when applied to June, whose flesh is merely flesh, without the self-awareness that elevates (although it can also demean) the thinking human being. Incapable of experience, June becomes like meat. Implicitly, her body is sustained in the realm of the human only by Amy's attention. When Jack loses his humanity to death, Amy takes formal leave of both her husband and her daughter, sadly relinquishing the "un-human" June to the kind of effective death her life has been for fifty years: "What I'm trying to say is Goodbye June. Goodbye Jack. They seem like one and the same thing" (278).

The importance of meat in *Last Orders*, and its close association with human flesh, recalls Swift's strong concern in *Waterland* with the differences and similarities between the human and the animal. In the earlier novel, the eel functions as a symbol of unselfconscious organicism, and is identified with Tom Crick's mentally handicapped brother, Dick. Like June, Dick Crick has no knowledge of time and no historical sense. He lives in time like a fish in water, and can bring no understanding to the mere fact of his physical existence. Both Dick and June are "accidental" children, born mentally challenged, and both are associated with the unknowing processes of natural life. The more fully human life-form, in both *Waterland* and *Last Orders*, is marked by mind and spirit, desire, and an irresistible analytical sense: what Tom Crick calls "curiosity." It is this curiosity which makes the human being an historical creature, obsessed with logic and cause and effect, while our bodies link us more closely to the animal world and the cyclicality of nature's movements. For this reason, the relationship between mother and child—particularly between mother and mentally handicapped child—is especially strong in Swift's work. Amy has watched over June faithfully for fifty years while Jack consistently refused to acknowledge his flesh and blood: "That was Jack's major failing, [Amy] said, that he didn't want to know his own daughter" (171).

Jack Dodds, Master Butcher, is a symbol in the novel of the human search for splendor in ashes. His body is both elevated and reduced by death, gaining in dignity but losing in materiality—the sheer bulk which marked him. All the characters in *Last Orders* are preoccupied with Jack's body—particularly his size. Holding the jar in the Coach at the start of the novel, Ray speculates: "And if it *is* Jack, whether it's really all of him or only what they could fit in the jar, him being a big bloke" (4). Ray traces his wartime friendship with Jack to the discrepancy in their physical sizes and the solidity of Jack, which comforted and protected Ray: "It was Jack who underwrote me. It wasn't that I was small so the bullets would miss me, it was that he was big, like a wall, like a boulder. And the bullets missed him anyway, they missed him so they missed me, except that once" (88).

Partly because of his size and the generosity that accompanies it, Mandy accepts Jack as a parent-figure as soon as she meets him in the cafeteria at Smithfield Market: "I never thought that an hour from then I'd be carried off to my future, to the rest of my life, in a butcher's van. By a big, round-armed, round-edged, big-voiced man who was like some uncle I never knew I had, who was like some man on the spot who'd been waiting specially for me to arrive" (162). Amy recalls how, at Wick's Farm, she was first drawn to Jack's large physique, and how his body spoke to hers in the "universal language" of flesh: "He was a muscle man too, a big man. . . . I don't mind admitting, that's how I liked 'em, or thought I did, big hunks of men. What more could a girl want than a big hunk of man? And I knew he had his eyes on me, down there on the next row of bins, I knew he had his feelers out" (235).

Jack's large body comes to represent the human body in a broader, emblematic sense in the novel. He stands for the strengths and weaknesses of the flesh, and speaks for the equalizing capacity of the body. Like death itself, flesh is a leveler, powerfully cutting through the fragile hierarchies of social order: Ray remembers "what Jack said in the desert, that we're all the same underneath, officers and ranks, all the same material. Pips on a man's shoulders don't mean a tuppenny toss" (28). Given his impressive size, the drama of Jack's death is a deeply affecting one. In the hospital, he loses his physical power as his body "packs up"; even his face is "all hollow with the flesh hanging on it" (34). His reduction to a jar of ashes underlines mortality emphatically in the novel, for there was something momentous, even heroic, in Jack's physique. Vic recalls asking him once what kind of tomb he would choose, and Jack replied: "Ooh, I don't know if you'd be up to it, Vic. I'm thinking big. I reckon nothing short of a pyramid" (197). Jack's choice here captures both his big ego and his sense of humor—that combination of arrogance and self-irony which Browne ascribes to humankind in the novel's first epigraph—as he jokes about claiming in death the prominence which the ancient Egyptian pharaohs sought in their massive, above-ground crypts.

In this regard, it's important that Jack is cremated rather than buried in *Last Orders*. The ancient Egyptian modes of burial referred to in the novel suggest an attitude towards the body and death which is contrary to that implied by cremation. Pyramids sought both to celebrate and to defy death by establishing the ongoing visibility of the dead person, and enlarging him symbolically to spectacular proportions. Huge and immobile, a pyramid seeks eternal presence for the dead, defying the evanescence of the body and attempting in some ways to deny mortality itself. Jack and Ray saw the pyramids together while serving in Egypt during World War II. Their friendship was born in a land of tombs, at a time of struggle and death for the world itself. The rootedness and stolidity of Jack Dodds, who never moved from the family butcher shop after returning from the war, is echoed—along with his self-importance—in the image of the pyramid. But the latter also works ironically in the novel. Even though they still stand, the pyramids bear testament to the inability of humans to defeat death. Built to defy mortality, the great mausoleums of the pharaohs in fact express death as inescapable, a conqueror. They speak indirectly of the anonymity and dissolution of the body, proclaiming the flesh as effectively ash, even while seeking to replace it with stone.

The pyramids, subject to the wear and tear of history and time, undo the very heroism they try to preserve. Jack's remains, unlocated in the earth, are subject to the same fate. Deceased, Jack, who chose never to budge from Bermondsey, acquires a mobility which an entombed or buried body could never possess. Immovable in life, Jack Dodds travels in death, eventually leaving the earth itself — first in a kind of flight, as his ashes are taken by the wind, and then for the water, as they are flung into the sea. In *Last Orders*, as in *Waterland*, the sea is the element which stands for both birth and death, the basic stations of the human journey. The sea is the place where the linear movement of historical time and the circular motion of organic time meet harmoniously. Vic, formally a sailor, describes the sea as "what makes all men equal for ever and always. There's only one sea" (143). The novel's second epigraph is a line from a popular song: "I do like to be beside the seaside." The conventional association here of the sea with holiday pleasure reinforces Jack's wish — expressed to Vic in a more serious mood — that he "wouldn't mind being buried at sea" (227). The sea offers comfort and a kind of peace to the body in death. It even recaptures, at life's end, a brief intimation of childhood happiness, while also offering the promise of devolution and a release from the body. Opening the jar on Margate Pier, Ray remarks that Jack's ashes are "like white soft sand on a beach" (294).

Last Orders elaborates the human body not just through images of meat and flesh, which establish its earthiness, but also through images of flight, which express its ethereality and spiritual properties. At the start of the novel, Ray describes sitting with Amy "in the garden by St. Thomas's, opposite Big Ben," reading the letter containing Jack's last orders (14). Amy talks of Jack's idea about the two of them retiring to a bungalow at Margate and becoming "new

people" at last (15). At the end of this monologue, the impossibility
of such newness and the finality of death is symbolically countered
by Ray's metaphor of the scavenging pigeons as "scatterings of ashes,
bits of ashes with wings" (16). The image of winged ash recurs at
the very end of the novel, as the seagulls wheel around the men
while they empty the urn. This imagery, bringing together flight
and ash, expresses the fervent hope for regeneration and new life—
for beginnings discovered within endings—which pervades *Last
Orders*. This hope informs the novel's religious references and gath-
ers in the beautiful descriptions of Canterbury Cathedral. It under-
pins the passionate love affairs of Jack and Amy, Ray and Amy, and
Vince and Mandy. It focuses tenaciously in Amy's love for June,
and quietly shapes the balanced serenity of Vic, the novel's priest-
figure—whose very name, Victor, suggests the victory, not just of
death, but also of love over despair.

All the characters, except Vic, long for the possibility of newness,
for fresh starts, and the chance to become "new people." Jack wants
a new life in Margate; Ray contemplates taking Amy on a trip to see
his daughter in Australia; Lenny and Vince both consider patching
up their differences with their children; Amy's visits to June constitute a protracted act of hope over many years. While the novel does
not unequivocally assert the viability of such a hope, its images of
the body transformed imply the potential for positive change—if
only in a metaphysical sense, on the other side of death. The
lightness of ash gives it a propensity for flight; Jack's metaphorically
winged remains suggest the discarding of the heavy flesh and the
flight of the soul beyond death. Ray compares throwing the ashes to
"scattering seed," and he describes the other three men "holding
their hands out cupped and tight like they've each got little birds to
set free" (293). The images of sowing and birds emphasize vitality
and resurrection as a possibility—even if unconfirmed—at the end
of the novel.

In this regard, "Lucky" Johnson assumes prominence as a figure not just of hope, but of the possibility of miracles. With his extraordinary good fortune as a punter, Ray embodies the chance that resurrection and new beginnings might manifest themselves on this side of the grave, not only for the dead but for the living. Ray seems to grasp life through his experience of being lucky. He accepts his luck as a gift and never questions it—although, like all providential gifts, it can sometimes be a hindrance. Charged with making Jack's final bet, Ray thinks: "It's a terrible burden having all this luck" (220). As his name and his small body suggest, "Lucky" is both weightless—spiritual, a ray of light—and heavy, for he has carried, at various times, the fate of the others on his shoulders. It was Ray who won the money for Lenny to finance his daughter's abortion, and it is Ray who wins the small fortune that will buy Jack out of his debt to loan sharks and provide for Amy's future. He shares a little of the Christly properties that cling to Dick Crick, the saintly brother, in *Waterland*.

Ray's luck is an expression in the novel of God's mysterious grace, which is, for Swift, as deeply rooted in the world and human life as suffering, loss, bewilderment, and death. Ray's love of horses is almost religious, and his luck seems a kind of reward for his deep appreciation of life's power and beauty. What motivates him as a gambler is not always winning; "Sometimes" he declares, "its just the glory of a horse" (259). Ray's love for Amy and the affair they have in their middle-age comes from this same appreciation: "But there's a beauty in that itself, I reckon, that's a lovable thing, fading beauty, it depends on your attitude" (170). The summer during which Amy spends Thursday afternoons in Ray's camper at Epsom race track instead of with June is a kind of new beginning—if only briefly—for both of them. And the monologue in which the discreet Vic confesses to having seen them leaving the Home together is one of the most moving in the novel: "It seemed to me that though they made the shapes of two separate people sitting on the same bench, so you might have thought it was just a chance encounter, they also made a single shape that was the two of them together" (216).

Appropriately, the runner that Ray backs in an effort to redeem the dying Jack's debts is an outsider named *Miracle Worker*. The horse, in a joyous affirmation of its name, wins effortlessly. Throughout the trip to Margate, Ray is carrying the thirty-four thousand pounds that he has won with the thousand pounds originally lent to Jack by Vince. This is significant, for the money is itself a gift—virtually, Ray's "child"—identifying Ray, rather than Vince, as the custodian of the future. Although Vince represents the younger generation and Ray the older, it is the latter who (literally) bears the promise of redemption: Ray has the means to a "new life" stuffed into his jacket pocket. Although we never learn what Ray does with the money, the fact that the novel's unlikely— because small, unobtrusive—"hero" has it is reassuring to the reader. Ray, "pregnant" with luck and money, symbolically replaces Jack at the novel's end and becomes a figure of annunciation. We recall the catch-all compliment paid to him by the Egyptian prostitute during the war. Alluding to Ray's physical and metaphysical gifts, she observes: "Little man, big cuck." " 'Well, Raysy,' " laughs Jack, " 'that sounds like just about everything rolled into one. Including luck' " (92). The good fortune of "Lucky" Johnson maintains, at the end of *Last Orders*, the ray of hope that breaks through the darkness of Swift's fictional worlds.

PARENTS AND CHILDREN

Hope usually manifests itself, for Swift, in the form of annunciatory metaphors and reworked references to Christ's miraculous birth.

The Christian myth provides him with a versatile model of beginnings and endings, new life, redemption, and sacrifice. In *Waterland*, for example, Dick Crick is called "The Savior of the World," and his giving of his life to save his cursed family suggests Christ's martyrdom for humankind's sins. The body is, of course, crucial to this myth's range of meanings, and it is through the body that *Last Orders* articulates its central theme of time and its vision of history. For Swift, the family and family relations constitute the vehicle for portraying both the passage of the body through time, and the embroilment of the human being in history. Specifically, for Swift (as for Dickens), the relationships between parents and children provide a way to investigate psychology, sexuality, and genealogy. Like Faulkner, Swift also uses parent/child relationships to articulate the political dimension of his work: a consideration of England's situation in the contemporary world.

As I have suggested, Swift's work presents both miracle and tragedy as inescapable aspects of human life. In this (as in other ways), it reveals its involvement with Shakespeare's *King Lear*, a tragedy about age and death, intergenerational conflict, family attachments, inheritance, and the fate of England. The connection between fathers and sons is very powerful in *Last Orders*, at both the literal and symbolic levels. Vince, as we have seen, disrupts the family line of inheritance by refusing to enter the butcher's trade, while Vic's sons dutifully assume their traditional role. In this regard, Vince represents a younger generation of Englishmen, who missed the primal bonding experience of World War II, and have no sense of the sacrifices that Jack's generation made for its country. Vince, Jack's adopted son, is rather like the unscrupulous Edmund, Gloucester's bastard son, in *King Lear*. Both men redefine filial duty as self-interest; each desires to exploit his father while holding the older, more credulous man at an emotional distance. Vince seeks a kind of genealogical distance from Jack as well, for he is reluctant to see himself as a Dodds, rejecting the name of the father as well as his profession: "I wasn't going to be no Vince Dodds," he tells Amy, "I wasn't going to be no butcher's boy" (159).

In addition, Vince's choice of cars instead of meat as a career expresses Swift's sense of England's younger generation as deracinated and mobile, unlike their immovably anchored parents. Ray's daughter, Susie, depicts this most clearly when she leaves England, marrying an Australian who had come to England merely to "visit" his roots in Somerset before returning to Sydney. Susie's departure destroys the Johnson family, as Carol leaves Ray soon afterwards. The broken family is a powerful image in Swift's work for disrupted historical (and geographical) continuity, and the emotional isolation of human beings.

The strongest echo of *King Lear* in *Last Orders* is in the troubled relationships between its fathers and daughters. Jack's rejection of June, Ray's disconnection from Susie, Lenny's abandonment of Sally, and Vince's trading of Kath to the wealthy Hussein collectively recall Lear's abandonment of Cordelia and attempted exploitation of her sisters Goneril and Reagan. This betrayal of the daughter by her father is the most intimate and tragic betrayal portrayed in Swift's work. It undermines the family by weakening the invisible ties of flesh and blood, and erasing the notion of duty. It undermines tradition by destroying lines of succession, and it strikes at the roots of love and hope. One manifestation of this falsity is father/daughter incest—a betrayal of the younger generation by the older which nevertheless has its counterpart in the child's betrayal of the father. Vince defects from the organic world to the mechanical one in his repudiation of Jack; Ray experiences Susie's departure as a kind of desertion.

This knot of mutual disloyalty encapsulates Swift's historical despair. It crystallizes in *Last Orders* as the anxiety the fathers feel about whether their offspring will come to their funerals, willing to do a child's final duty and execute their last orders. Swift's older, tormented protagonists—like Tom Crick, Ray, and Lenny—struggle to learn from their mistakes, and to pass on such lessons to the next generation as wisdom. Yet Swift sees the generations caught in a cycle of weakness and failure, unable to fully communicate with each other, and thus unable to improve the world: "I reckon every generation makes a fool of itself for the next one" (43), thinks Lenny.

In the light of this apparent entrapment in frailty, the idea of beginnings, fresh starts, and idealized origins appeals strongly to the imaginations of Swift's characters: "I reckon every generation wants the next one to make it all come better," continues Lenny, "to make it seem like there's a second chance" (44). The Fall is alluded to frequently in Swift's fictions. In *Last Orders*, the scene of humanity's fall from grace into a world of death and labor is Wick's Farm, "the Garden of England," where Jack and Amy played Adam and Eve. The expulsion from the garden is signaled by the birth of June and the symbolic death of her parents' marriage—depicted in the novel as Jack's throwing of the teddybear he won for Amy off the jetty at Margate. Swift's characters are subject to repetition—intergenerational, historic, and mythic. The tossing of the teddy bear not only foreshadows the "chucking" (19) of Jack himself off the pier, it also mimes his rejection of June and the betrayal of the future which this rejection involves.

The betrayal of the daughter—requiring as it does a concomitant betrayal of her mother—stands, in fact, for the (fore)father's betrayal of futurity itself. It is echoed again in the novel in Lenny's poignant meditation on Sally and Vince's aborted child. Recalling his duty to kill in the war, Lenny asks himself: "What's one little unborn sod who aint ever going to see the light of day?" Then he names himself by his soldier's title: "Gunner Tate" (204). Just as Jack Dodds, family butcher, butchered his own family by repudiating June, so Lenny assumes Lear's mantle of misguided fatherhood; he sees his insistent paternal power as responsible for the loss of Sally's child and the destruction of his daughter's life.

For Swift, the aborted child becomes the ultimate sacrifice — a victim of humanity's loss of faith in the future, and a tragic sign of paternal failure. After the catastrophe of sexual knowledge in the Garden, the "lost" child comes to signify the degeneration of the body — its ontological conversion to meat, and all that that suggests of humanity's deep, redemptive need for "lambs to the slaughter." The aborted child is the life that is "chucked" to make way for other lives, wishes, and stories. It functions as an apocalyptic emblem: its interrupted development signifies the miscarriage of time itself and the destruction of history's possibilities. In *Last Orders*, June Dodds (again like Dick Crick) is effectively an aborted child, a sacrificial lamb. Although she is named for springtime — "JuneJuneJune" (277) — life and futurity cannot spring from June, just as nothing can be built on the curtailed form of Vince and Sally's child.

In this regard, unconventional family relations stand in Swift's work for a kind of historical timidity: a generational failure of nerve, and a veiled wish to stop time itself. Incest is a recurring motif in his fictions, particularly between fathers and daughters, which Tom Crick describes as "like tying up into a knot the thread that runs into the future" (*Waterland*, 197). Watching Susie dry her hair, Ray admits: "It's still true that if I were a different man, a younger one, if my name was Andy and I came from Sydney, Australia, then I'd fancy Sue, like I fancied Carol, only more. I'd fancy my own daughter" (51). Vince and Mandy express primarily the importance of incest in *Last Orders*. Mandy sees Vince — and even Jack, briefly — as a figure both sexual and paternal, a pattern repeated in her daughter Kath's connection to the older Hussein. Mandy also responds to Vince as a kind of brother: "we were somehow, underneath it all, like *brother* and *sister*, worse, father and daughter," enacting in Ray's camper a parodic version of the paradise myth: Vince was just "back from the Middle East, 'from the bleeding garden of Aden, sweetheart' " (157, emphasis in original). Sibling incest is echoed in Vince's earlier association with his surrogate sister, Sally Tate, and in Amy's affair with Ray, who is set up in the novel as a kind of brother to Jack, and who replaces him in Amy's affection.

In Swift's work, father/daughter incest articulates the betrayal of the daughter by the father not through rejection, but through an excess of acceptance and intimacy. It also enacts their mutual turning away from the future towards a fantasy of regressive idealism. In *Last Orders*, incest functions as a secret dream of time's suspension — of the body preserved from time's ravages through a doubling back to its own origins. Incest seeks to circumvent linear motion, and even to defeat death, by reinstating a primal innocence of origination and recreating, in this phantasmal way, the prelapsarian world. It is no accident that one of the geographically and historically distant lands evoked in the novel is ancient Egypt: a society longing to defy death, in which incest was an acceptable part of dynastic politics.

Clearly, Swift's characters move within narratives of primordial repetition: the Fall, the miraculous birth, the ancient story of betrayal, sacrifice and resurrection, the taboo. Ordinary people tested by life, his characters take on mythic lineaments themselves: the Temptress, the Mother, the Innocent. Such archetypes suggest again the influence on Swift of the Victorian realists — Thomas Hardy in particular, with his stark reworkings of Greek tragedy. Swift's view of modernity is shaped (like Hardy's) by the cyclicality of history and myth — as well as the endless recycling of old narratives through the collective unconscious of the race. Reading his work, we cannot help but feel that the more things change the more they stay the same. As Vince says to Mandy in the camper: "We'll have to stay put and scarper at the same time." When she asks how, he replies "Motors" (160). It is this haunted sense of motion as in some ways futile that undermines the freedom the younger genera-tion looks for in its automobiles. At Margate, even Vince must leave his "mate" (73), the blue Mercedes, at the curb, become a son, and perform his father's last orders: "Go on, Vincey, go on" Ray urges him on the Pier, "And he takes a scoop" (293).

Swift brings the same kind of universal awareness to places as he does to characters in his work. Many of his settings are archetypal as well as highly individualized. In *Last Orders*, Canterbury Cathe-dral, as we have seen, is both an historically-specific site and a spiritual place — a threshold space where different realms connect and humans can sense God. Similarly, Margate is both a seedy, out-of-season holiday resort and a mythic place of oceanic timelessness, of dreams and departures. Other locations which Swift makes uni-versally applicable to human needs and desires are the butcher's shop, the undertaker's slab, the lavatory, and the pub. The former two, as I have implied, represent the lowest-common-denominator sites of life and death. The lavatory is likewise a place of basic need, effectively leveling distinctions among people, and providing emo-tional as well as physical relief. It is almost a kind of church. At Rochester, Ray goes to the "Gents" both to urinate and weep while meditating on life and the passage of time. The lavatory also offers a piquant, unpretentiously honest perspective on the world: "There's always a frosted quarter-light, chinked open, with a view of the back end of somewhere, innyards, alleyways, with some little peephole out on life" (112). Like the pubs at which the men stop along their way, the lavatory is a structural emblem for humanity itself: at once profane and holy, it suggests both waste and glory, the baseness of the body and its truthfulness.

The final spokesman in the novel for this insoluble mixedness of the human creature is Jack's deceased father, Ronnie Dodds — who speaks to us through the memory of his son, from a strange remove beyond death, and who reminds us that "the nature of the goods," of meat and man, "is perishable" (285). In the face of such perishability, Swift implies, faith provides a possible counter-narrative of eternity. The discourse of the spirit begins in the places where the body breaks down: places of water, of drinking, and excretion, like pubs and "pissers" (112); and places of stone, of tombs and rigidity, like cathedrals and monuments. Miracle begins, so Swift intimates, at the outermost limits of history—where cause and effect dissolve, and the image of four men scattering ashes shapes itself into a modern hieroglyph.

The sobering view from the lavatory window reminds Ray of all the racetracks he's been to, and, on this basis, he constructs "the map of England with the roads criss-crossing. AscotBrighton-CheltenhamDoncasterEpsom" (112). *Last Orders* similarly builds up a picture or map of England—its geography and culture—through the familiar popular referents of racetracks and pubs, memorials, churches, towns, and London with its famous buildings, like Big Ben and the Old Bailey. As in *The Remains of the Day*, the travelers in *Last Orders* explore an England both changing and oddly timeless, caught between a present of dwindled power and a past which lingers as cultural myth. Swift ends his novel where Ishiguro ends *Remains*: at the very limit of the land, on a pier jutting into the sea—which suggests the unknown future of a once-powerful country uncertain of its role in the post-imperial world. Reprising ironically the traditional colonial metaphor of center and margin, Swift casts London as the metropolitan hub; but his characters proclaim Smithfield, not Trafalgar Square or Whitehall, as the city's real core. Ray expresses the popular perception that "Smithfield was the true centre, the true heart of London. Bleeding heart, of course, on account of the meat. How Smithfield wasn't just Smithfield, it was Life and Death. . . . So what you had in Smithfield was your three Ms: Meat, Medicine and Murders" (26).

This image of the bloody heart of London contrasts poignantly with the august yet cliché image of Kent as "the Garden of England." When the men stop at Wick's Farm, Ray describes the view of the countryside as panoramic — "like we're standing on the rim of a big, crooked bowl" — in contrast to the cramped view from a lavatory's "quarter-light": "Down in the valley it's all green and brown and patchy, woods marked off with neat edges and corners, hedges like stitching. There's a splodge of red brick in the middle with a spire sticking up. It looks like England, that's what it looks like" (145). In this brief evocation of a landscape out of Wordsworth or Gainsborough, Swift casts post-imperial Britain as a place caught up in representations: in residual myths both brutal and nostalgic. Contemporary England becomes a place unsure of and seeking its historical mission — the "true" meanings of its past and future — just as the four men are unsure of and seeking the "true" meanings of their complex errand.

In the novels of Swift and Ishiguro, England seems to hover on the edge of an undefined, still-unfolding modernity, tempted both to fling itself forward (like the plucky remains of Jack Dodds) and to retreat (like Ishiguro's butler, Mr. Stevens) into the glazed decor of an embalmed past. The political question that *Last Orders* phrases echoes that of *The Remains of the Day*. It is an urgent one for contemporary British novelists: can England — with its antiquated systems of social hierarchy, its almost-extinct languages of class distinction — adapt and move on to "the next world" of the twenty-first century? Graham Swift's answer remains ambivalent.

3

The Novel's Reception

Last Orders was well-received by critics, in both Britain and the United States, when it first appeared. Reviewers were quick to respond to the novel's technical virtuosity, astute portraiture, and compelling emotional strength. In the *Times Literary Supplement* of 19 January 1996, Oliver Reynolds spoke of Swift as a kind of Hardyian sage, respecting his characters and deftly finding the universal within the particular: "*Last Orders* is about how we live and how we die and our struggle to make abiding connections between the two." Reynolds praised the work as a wonderful example of "the novel's power to resolve the wavering meanings of the life we all share into a definite focus, one where the clarity with which things are seen renders them precious." Reynolds was most impressed by Swift's multilayered technique, especially the "concision" of Swift's method, "simultaneously sparse and weighty," and the parity he creates among the characters: "They each tell Jack's story in their own way and thus tell the story of their own lives."

Many critics sounded a similarly enthusiastic note. In the *New York Times* of 11 April 1996, Christopher Lehmann-Haupt praised Swift for departing from the Jamesian tones of his earlier works and finding a convincingly colloquial idiom in *Last Orders*. He compared the novel to the "Hades" chapter of Joyce's *Ulysses*, where the Dubliners attend the funeral of Paddy Dignam. Lehmann-Haupt also singled out, as several commentators did, the novel's poignant portrayal of "a dying generation bonded and shaped by World War II." Jay Perini, in a review entitled "Canterbury Tale" which appeared in the *New York Times Book Review* on 5 May 1996, called *Last Orders* a novel of "impeccable authenticity," and described Swift's "most vivid accomplishment" as "the tumbling cockney used by his characters." In order to create such fine ventriloquism, Perini argued, a writer must have "perfect pitch": the ability to simulate dialect without condescending to his characters. Like many other critics, Perini found Swift's ability to turn the ordinary into the mythic persuasive and moving.

Perhaps the strongest and most glowing response to the novel came from John Banville in his review "That's Life!", which appeared in the *New York Review of Books* on 4 April 1996. Banville described Swift as "one of England's finest living novelists," praising in particular his "unfussy subtlety of style, sly wit, and deep humanistic strain." If Swift's writing lacks "fieriness," Banville averred, it makes up for this by a compassionate awareness of the pain of living, "an awareness that, in the best of his work, swells into an authentic and at times magisterial tragic sense." After commenting on Swift's fine handling of the war as an ambiguous referent for British national identity, Banville called Swift very "English" in his concern with the family as *the* social unit for the novelist's examination. Using the kind of genealogical image favored by Swift himself in his fiction, Banville described the latter as the heir — more so than Martin Amis or Julian Barnes — of the "great Victorians." He concluded his review by applying to Swift a phrase of John Dewey's, praising Emerson as the "sage of ordinary days."

Last Orders was equally popular with readers, selling well from the start, and, after Swift received the Booker Prize in October 1996, it became a bestseller on both sides of the Atlantic. Critical responses to the novel remained highly positive in the wake of the award. However, the success of *Last Orders* was slightly shadowed by the controversy over the validity of the Booker prize itself, and by the unease at Swift's many references to Faulkner's *As I Lay Dying*.

The day after Swift received the prize, novelist V. S. Naipaul denounced it passionately to London's *Evening Standard* newspaper: "The Booker is murder. . . . It is useless. I have no regard for it at all. . . . No one knows what a novel is any more — it is all foolish. All novels written now are debris — new characters in old work." Naipaul's condemnation was unexpectedly seconded by one of the five Booker Prize judges, A. N. Wilson, in an equally denunciatory column in the *Evening Standard*: "I have spent the past six months reading 150 novels for the Booker," he complained. "The great majority were of no quality at all. . . . The Booker died ages ago, and it is now running around like a farmyard chicken with no head." In response to both Naipaul and Wilson, the chair of the judges, Carmen Calill, made a speech defending the prize against the "obsessive denigration of English fiction," which she described as "the dying chirrup of some sort of imperial misery." In the midst of this luridly-worded controversy, sales of *Last Orders* rose steadily.

The issue of Swift's indebtedness to Faulkner precipitated arguments among critics. John Flow, as mentioned earlier, found the allusions offensive, given that *Last Orders* was, in his opinion, "pointless and flabby." However, Claire Messud, who had reviewed the novel for the *Times*, found Swift's reworking of *As I Lay Dying* compelling. She described *Last Orders* as "a triumphant and ultimately redemptive adaptation of Faulkner's classic," and "a resonant

work of art in its own right." Amongst various arguments to the
effect that "good" borrowing was a fine strategy while "bad" borrowing was not, the two Booker judges whom the press approached for
comment—Ian Jack and Jonathan Coe—admitted that the comparison with Faulkner had not occurred to them, neither having read
As I Lay Dying.

Whatever the effect of controversies such as these on the literary
and cultural meanings of a work, they fuelled the critical perspective of Swift's detractors, who saw the very strengths of *Last Orders*,
as summarized above, as signs of the novel's weakness. It was precisely Swift's resemblance to the time-honored, "Victorian sage"
image of wisdom that certain critics found objectionable. In her
review entitled "Heart of Bermondsey" (*New Statesman and Society*,
19 January 1996), Ruth Pavey expressed doubts about the verisimil-
itude of Swift's depiction of a working-class environment. *Last Orders*, Pavey observed, begins in the vernacular mode of the popular
British television series *EastEnders*, but it soon modulates into a
Chekhovian drama: "a delicate mix of warmth and humour with
sad, constraining disappointment." She praised Swift for "his ability
to create an encompassing feeling, a sense of his novels existing in
their own special air"; but she also criticized him for depicting a
"hermetic" Bermondsey, unrealistically sealed off from the multi-
cultural society surrounding it. Pavey described Swift's view of Bermondsey as "very partial," and essentially out of touch with the
troubled history of the former docking community in the 1980s.
She concluded: "Swift has again created a bewitching impression
of place, but it is an imaginary one . . . more a Bermondsey of the
heart than of actual experience."

Pavey's reading of *Last Orders* argues for a kind of distance from
working-class experience which Swift maintains, despite the intimate quality of his character-drawing. Other critics picked up the
suggestion of an elitist perspective adopted in the novel. Melissa

Bennetts in the *Christian Science Monitor* of 27 February 1997, found it "disconcerting" that *Last Orders* has an intellectual writer imagining the working class, "rather than an accurate representation of their speech and lives." To this end, she criticized Swift for not differentiating clearly among the characters in terms of speech styles. This issue of differentiation troubled other commentators as well. While critics like Jay Perini admired Swift's ventriloquism, even John Banville felt that the characters' voices were too similar, and that the different generations, both younger and older, spoke — remarkably — in much the same way.

These criticisms argue for Swift's assumption of a sage-like moral superiority towards, and class-based distance from, the ensemble cast he creates in *Last Orders*. Other critics, as we have seen, praised Swift for what they saw as precisely his *lack* of condescension towards his characters. Such diametrically opposite views were also expressed with regard to Swift's technique in the novel. While Reynolds et al admired the technical ease and narrative fluency of *Last Orders*, James Bowman in the *National Review* (10 March 1997) condemned Swift's style as "modish"; both he and Bennetts also read the novel's plot reductively as "daytime soap opera." Although Bowman conceded that the story remained "affecting" despite its triteness, he dismissed *Last Orders* rather savagely, as a sign of the cultural bankruptcy and political narcissism of our postmodern times: "Martin Walker says that Bill Clinton is 'the president we deserve,' and maybe, in the self-absorbed and complacent 1990s, this is the fiction we deserve."

The broad critical differences outlined here can perhaps be read as mixed responses to Swift's ambivalences as a novelist. His roots are strongly, as I've suggested, in the realist fiction of the nineteenth-century, and he draws extensively on the Victorian novel for structure, image, and theme in his work. Yet he also transposes modernist experimentation and postmodern narrative self-consciousness onto the assumptions of nineteenth-century realism. John Fowles did the same kind of playing with older paradigms in his work of the 1960s and 1970s, and his novels drew similarly polarized reactions of admiration and outrage from critics. Like Fowles, Swift remains elusive of categories—in some ways a "traditional" English novelist in the mode of Dickens, but bringing to the familiarity of Victorian fictional conventions the structural unease of modernism, and the artistic disillusion of postmodernity. Thus while certain critics see Swift as too conservative a novelist to speak eloquently for our times, others see him as a prisoner of fashion— radical to the point of "modishness"—and over-involved with academic theories of the novel.

Among those critics who attacked Swift for his narrow view of society and the implied elitism of his "humanistic strain" was Nicholas Tredell, who wrote a scathing article, "Feelgood Fiction," in the Spring 1997 issue of the *Oxford Quarterly*. Tredell picked up the linguistic/ethical issue of speaking for the working class in his criticism of Swift's use of the interior monologue: "Swift's mimicry might be interpreted as a defense mechanism, for it is possible that if people like those whom he purports to represent did speak for themselves, they might say more challenging, more uncomfortable things than he permits them to." Tredell's objections are based on his sense of Swift as politically out of touch; the fiction, he avers, excludes "feminists, gays, and ethnic minorities" while focusing excessively on Britain's "problematic glories," the Industrial Revolution and World War II.

Tredell's article represents certain critical reservations about *Last Orders* taken to an extreme. Against it we might put the glowing remarks of John Benrose in his review, "A Long Day's Journey into Life and Death," for *Maclean's* (6 April 1996). Comparing Swift to Breughel in his apt depictions of the lives of ordinary people, Benrose describes the novel as august in its scope and "masterful": "He has never before woven history so artfully into the texture of the present — the ghosts of the past taking their rightful, disturbing place in the minds of the living. In *Last Orders*, the little people who lived the big events receive a fit and moving commemoration." It is important to remember, however, that Swift, like Ishiguro, has set himself the difficult task of portraying England in the aftermath of the imperial project, at a time of changing definitions of national identity, and the radical demythologizing of place. In the cultural context of late twentieth-century Britain, Swift's regionalism is bound to be troubled, for the very endeavor of representing England is under scrutiny. In the light of arguments over what "England" is, who should claim it, and which "England" should be represented in art, critical accusations against Swift for portraying an "imaginary" England should be taken seriously.

It is equally worthwhile to remember what Swift himself has said about the crucial role of the imagination in a writer's oeuvre: "I have enormous faith in the imagination. If your imagination cannot transport you mentally from where you are to somewhere quite different, then don't be a novelist, be something else." The writer's task, Swift declares, is to move beyond familiar horizons, through acts of imaginative projection, "into other experiences that become yours as you write." This, for Swift is the risk, the "leap into the unknown" that the writer owes to his/her creativity. We might interpret this belief in the imagination politically, as a vindication of the novelist as ventriloquist — *obliged* to "speak for the other" as part of his/her craft: "Your own life, your own experience, provides you with only limited fuel," Swift told *Maclean's*. "And the imagination has to do the rest of your work. I think the imagination is a marvelous kind of mental transportation. It can take you to new and exciting places." Swift's views here offer another perspective on the idea of an "imaginary" England, perhaps bringing him closer to the fantasists and magic realists — Rushdie, Winterson — from whom he also seems so remote.

John Benrose called *Last Orders* "a finer achievement than *Waterland*." John Banville spoke of the difficulties facing a writer who achieves great success with an early work and thus sets a standard for the books to follow. One of the challenges that Swift faced throughout the late 1980s and early 1990s was the comparison of his novels *Out of this World, Ever After,* and *Last Orders* to *Waterland*. The latter was enormously successful at the time of its appearance in 1983, earning great praise from critics and gaining wide popularity among readers. *Waterland* went on to bridge the traditional gap between a novel's general readership and the academy, for it was welcomed by literary scholars and soon became the focus of academic scholarship on Swift. Short-listed for the Booker, *Waterland* was also taken up by the cinema and made into a successful film. Neither *Out of this World* (1988) nor *Ever After* (1992) achieved the success of *Waterland*, although both novels were well-received by critics. *Last Orders*, however, has been very favorably compared to the earlier novel, and some critics see it as surpassing *Waterland* in its depth of vision and subtlety of emotion. In this regard, it's tempting to see the awarding of the Booker to *Last Orders* as a stamp of approval of sorts. Has the novel been officially designated a contemporary "classic," to an even greater extent than *Waterland* was? Its formal recognition by the literary establishment is to be accompanied by its popular apotheosis; like *Waterland, Last Orders* has been made into a film.

In reviews, one of the specific points of comparison between these two novels has been Swift's handling of his women characters. In his earlier works, women tend to be defined mostly through their involvement with men, and their stories are wrapped up within men's stories to an almost stifling degree. Mary Crick, so crucial to the unfolding of *Waterland*, never quite emerges in her own right, for her voice never stands alone, as it were. She does not tell her own story, Tom tells it for her. The female voice is heard more assertively in *Last Orders*, where the interior monologues project all voices as, in a sense, freestanding. Although the two main women characters, Amy and Mandy Dodds, live lives shaped by men, they have monologues of their own in the novel, and each eloquently describes her own emotion and experience.

Banville approvingly observes this shift in Swift's portrayal of women, for they cease to be just sounding-boards for the male characters or "handmaids to the plot." Ruth Pavey, however, finds Swift's reading of women less exhilarating, and quite contradictory. The disappointment which she sees as defining the characters' lives is based on failed love, unrealized ambitions, and unwelcome change. Women, she states, seem to have caused much of the trouble, especially daughters. But, Paley observes, the deepest disappointments depicted in *Last Orders* are those suffered by the women, and this subtle contradiction seems to indicate unresolved attitudes toward women in the novel. The relationships between women and men are key to Swift's concerns as a novelist, and he continues to explore their complexities, particularly in his handling of voice.

Finally, one of the criticisms leveled at *Last Orders* was for its darkness and negativity. Most critics responded to the novel as basically a hopeful, even life-affirming, work. Banville loved Swift's quiet reaffirmation of the traditional humanistic values of "decency loyalty, and love," while Claire Bose, writing in *Europe* (March 1997), admired the way in which a "deeply moving" and "thought-provoking tale never once falls into gloom or despondency." However, Gary Davenport, in the *Sewanee Review* (summer 1997), chose *Last Orders* as a good example of what he called the contemporary "novel of despair." Davenport argued that for earlier writers like

Tolstoy, Dostoevsky, Camus, Lawrence, and even Hardy, despair led eventually to hope, but the lack of any affirmation beyond the playing of narrative games is a postmodern phenomenon. Swift, Davenport states, is not only over-tricky in his technique, but presents human life as unremittingly hard, cruel, and deterministic. Such hardship can be endured if it is found to be meaningful, but "meaning is denied everywhere in *Last Orders*." The characters, for Davenport, have no real sense of historical context: the town of Rochester is reduced to a logo on a plastic bag; Canterbury Cathedral is a repellant edifice that seems to sneer at the travelers. Davenport sums up what he sees as the gloomy nihilism of the novel, tracing it to "an oppressive sense of transience without transcendence. . . . The few positive forces in the novel — camaraderie, for example, and a sort of graveyard humor — are neither able nor apparently intended to counter the general sense of despair."

Davenport's criticisms are worth taking seriously, for they resonate with the charges of pessimism which have been brought against Swift's other novels. Here the influence of *King Lear* on Swift's oeuvre is especially interesting, for *Lear* has been seen as Shakespeare's darkest tragedy. Its existential bleakness has prompted comparisons of the play with absurdist works of the twentieth-century, especially Samuel Beckett's *Endgame*. Despair is certainly an important part of Swift's fictional worlds, and it is precisely the sense of dread at an apparently empty universe which Swift takes so eloquently from *Lear* and from Shakespeare's classical forbears. But to claim despair as the dominant feature of the Swiftian universe is to over-simplify his enterprise as a writer. Swift's fiction works *between* possibilities, within and against tensions, maintaining a poised and thoroughgoing oscillation of opposites. Despair and hope are both parts of his work, as they are of the work of the tragedians he recalls; to emphasize only one is to distort the whole.

Most of the scholarly criticism on Swift deals with *Waterland*. *Last Orders*, still a relatively recent work, has not yet fully entered the academy and been processed through the mechanisms of scholarship. A website on Swift maintained by Brown University's George Landow includes only one article: "History and 'Englishness' in Graham Swift's *Last Orders*," by Heike Hartung-Bruckner. This essay, like the reviews and review articles discussed above, raises crucial questions about the novel — its content and structure, its relation to other contemporary novels, and its historical context as a work of late twentieth-century fiction. These issues suggest the richness of the novel, the rewards it offers to serious study, and the potential it has to entrance scholars as powerfully as it has engaged a wide range of other readers. Fans and students of *Last Orders*, as of Swift's work in general, have much to look forward too.

4

The Novel's Performance

Last Orders has been a bestseller in both Britain and the United States. As we have seen, it was well-reviewed by critics in both countries. In addition, Swift's popularity has grown steadily throughout much of the world since the publication of *Waterland*. His fictions are much-translated. The film of *Waterland*, starring Jeremy Irons as Crick, Sinead Cusack as Mary, and Ethan Hawke as the rebellious pupil, Price, was also popular and successful. Like Ishiguro, Swift has found a highly responsive audience for the vision of England he generates — a vision which appeals to both general and specialized readers, to fans of the novel as well as to literary scholars. In this chapter, I explore the appeal of Swift's vision, placing it in a wider context of certain novels and movies which also construct and market an image of the country. In the light of the recent movie version of *Last Orders*, I also elaborate here upon some aspects of Swift's work which make it attractive to the medium of film.

In *Last Orders*, there is an emphasis on views. The English countryside is presented to us, in a couple of memorable moments, from a painterly perspective, and we are encouraged to step back from the land and observe it. At Wick's Farm, Ray looks at the spread of fields, hedges, and woods and he sums up: "It looks like England, that's what it looks like. The field slopes up to the left, to a crest, where there's a clump of trees and, peeping up from the other side, a tar-brown stump of a building, a windmill, with its sails missing. . . . Near the gate the grass is trodden bare and sprinkled with sheep shit. There's a water trough tucked in by the hedge, galvanized metal. We can hear sheep and smell sheep and we can see them, dotted across the slope" (145–6). Here are all the components of the English pastoral scene, as many representations have given them to us: fields, rustic buildings, sheep. It's almost as if the landscape has posed itself photogenically for the curious eye of the — literary or armchair—traveler. We might think of, among others, Wordsworth, Constable, or Austen.

The invitation to the camera's eye is irresistible, and the scene recalls not just similar vistas in Thomas Hardy's novels, or the studied tableaus of landscape in Ishiguro's fiction, but filmic representations of those vistas. Swift adopts here the all-encompassing view that John Schlesinger adopted so eloquently in his 1968 film of *Far From the Madding Crowd*, or that Roman Polanski favored for his 1979 film of *Tess of The D'Urbervilles*. James Ivory also deftly set up the removed yet admiring painterly perspective on a serene countryside for his 1993 film version of *The Remains of the Day*. The appeal of such a ceremonious visual unfolding of England is the appeal of familiar resonances and the creation, for the observer, of a safe space of observation. Uninvolved, we may observe and enjoy beauty. The directors mentioned above—among whom we might include Ang Lee, with his reverent version of *Sense and Sensibility*—all exploited this perspective to paint England as rich, colorful, and gorgeous. This sense of England as photogenic and familiar, a kind of souvenir of an old world, is part of the success, in both print and film media, of novels like *The Remains of the Day* and *Waterland*.

The films of James Ivory and Ismail Merchant have perhaps gone further than any others in rendering England uncompromisingly picturesque. Their adaptations of E. M. Forster's novels, particularly the hugely popular *A Room with a View* and *Howards End*, combine the familiar images of English landscape painting and pastoral poetry with the glossy shallowness of calendar or travelogue photographs. The result is a pretty but hackneyed effect of pastoralism without texture, and of vista without depth. Even Merchant-Ivory's highly-praised film of *The Remains of the Day* erases much of the novel's complexity. Like Swift in *Last Orders*, Ishiguro subtly interrogates familiar ways of envisioning the English landscape and questions the meanings of its beauty. But James Ivory keeps to the dazzling, seductive surface of the image and the film has the glossy, exact feel of a television commercial.

For Swift, the poignancy of such a cliché rendition of England is its lifelessness, the absence of people it presupposes. In *Last Orders*, the lush landscape of Wick's Farm is more than a postcard; it is troubled and enlivened by the disordering plunge of human beings into its representational perfection. Vince remembers an earlier visit with his adoptive parents and Sally: "[Jack] stands and looks at the view. I think, It's because the sheep get killed. . . . The view's all far off and little and its as though we're far-off and little too. . . . He takes a deep breath, then another one, quick, and I reckon he wanted to change his mind, but he was already teetering, toppling, on top of that hill, and he couldn't stop himself" (65).

One alternative to the buff glamorizations of Merchant-Ivory is the blunt, politically charged naturalism of Neil Jordan. In films like *Mona Lisa* (1990) and *The Crying Game* (1992), Jordan seeks another idiom for Englishness, one which acknowledges the multiculturalism of the country's postcolonial citizenry. In Jordan's London—like that of writer/filmmaker Hanif Kureishi—texture dominates; street life establishes its own tough vocabulary of strong convictions, strong desires, and decisive actions. Violence and lust become a sort of common denominator for an England released from the decorums of Austen, James, and Forster. In such films, England in general and London in particular are sometimes seen as satanic and doomed—a fitting site for the end of the world. This apocalyptic tone can be read as a response to Britain's economic crisis in the wake of imperialism, and as a rather desperate reaction to the merciless social environment of the Thatcher years. At the same time, the decay and gloom of the last twenty years comes through as a kind of perverse glamour in classic movies of British grunge, like Kureishi's *My Beautiful Laundrette* and *Sammy and Rosie Get Laid*, *Withnail and I*, *Trainspotting*, and *My Son the Fanatic*.

Another alternative to the Merchant-Ivory approach is the work of Peter Greenaway. In his films of the '80s and '90s, like *The Draughtsman's Contract* and *The Cook, the Thief, his Wife and her Lover*, Greenaway parodies the conventions of high-bourgeois landscape and portrait painting, with images of lurid brutality in apparently safe and genteel settings. His films attempt a hard-headed yet sophisticated look at modern England's social anxieties and their roots in the history of the sixteenth and seventeenth centuries. In effect, Greenaway's films recoup much of the smoothness and elitism of the Merchant-Ivory style by trying to apply it inversely, from an unconvincingly low-life perspective. They celebrate the glamour of wealth and privilege while ostensibly debunking it.

It is easy to see how Swift's fiction might appeal to any one of these filmic approaches, for his vision of England includes a little of everything: the physical beauty so overstated by Merchant-Ivory, the graininess and conflict beloved of Jordan, the despair of Kureishi et al, and the troubled erudition of Greenaway. *Waterland*, however, avoided such co-opting. The film was directed by Stephen Gyllenhaal, and the casting of Jeremy Irons in the lead role was perhaps the only concession to the cultural mythology of an idealized Englishness. Irons had made his reputation as a sort of "professional Englishman," playing the hero in such high-brow classics as the TV miniseries *Brideshead Revisited*—a hit in the 1980s—and *The French Lieutenant's Woman*, for which Harold Pinter wrote the script. Irons was to the 1980s and early 1990s what Anthony Hopkins and Ralph Fiennes have since become—the embodiment of a certain mythic English manhood: fretful but poised, aloof yet sexy, smoldering but always polite.

The film of *Waterland* was, however, subject to the oversimplifications of the medium. As with *The Remains of the Day*, it proved impossible to capture the full scope of the novel's narrative subtlety on film. No matter how vivid his descriptions and imagery, Swift never sacrifices the power of the word for that of the picture. In film versions of novels, given the constraints of time, this is easy to do and perhaps inevitable. Moreover, the setting of *Waterland* was transferred to America, and the narrative converted into an insular drama of mournful expatriates. While this shift of setting does reflect the understated importance of America in Swift's work—the new world hovers always just beyond the old—the loss of England's geographical specificity robbed the story of its cultural frame and thus of its vitality. Although successful on its own terms, the film of *Waterland* distorted or erased the complexity of Swift's themes.

The film version of *Last Orders* is directed by Fred Schepisi, so it might escape some of the conventions of the "condition of England" movie outlined above. Schepisi's best-known film is *A Cry in the Dark*, which was sharply critical of Australian society and shaped the famous landscape of the outback as stark and commer-cialized. He also directed the film version of David Hare's play *Plenty*, which dealt with postwar disillusion in England and the shrinking of the country's political horizons. Schepisi's approach is spare but not brutal; his eye is satirical yet compassionate. He is able to integrate the romance and allure of film-making into his narratives, and to capture depth of character and space. He is an interesting choice for *Last Orders*, which is character-driven in many ways but also comments upon English social history, and the role of the individual life in the larger fabric of the country.

With its strong ensemble cast, well-paced action, dramatic inten-sity, emotional depth, and vivid language, *Last Orders* has much to recommend it to the filmmaker. The cast of performers that Schep-isi has assembled is a powerful one of mostly mature, much-admired British actors. Michael Caine plays Jack Dodds, with the other male roles being taken by Bob Hoskins (who appeared with Caine in *Mona Lisa*), Tom Courtenay, David Hemmings, and Ray Win-stone. Helen Mirren plays Amy. The film was shown at the Toronto International Film Festival in September 2001 and is due for gen-eral release in 2002.

Swift's novel appeared at a time, the mid-1990s, when England was a gripping subject in literature, television, and film. Since then, that fascination has, if anything, increased. The death of Princess Diana and the country's obsessive memorializing of her, the open-ing of new museums like Beamish, and the knighting of older performers like Sean Connery, Elton John, and Paul McCartney—as well as Caine himself—have emphasized mourning and the role of memory for an England in transition. They have invited recollec-tions and reexaminations of the country's recent past. Films like *The English Patient*, *In the Name of the Father*, *The Limey*, and *Sexy Beast* are works that depend on both mourning and memory—

they are, in a sense, memorials to or histories of the present—for they place England within the turbulent present while also revisiting its past.

The English Patient recalls both colonialism and World War II; *In the Name of the Father* revisits the history of terrorism in the "swinging" London of the 1960s and attacks the British legal establishment of that time. *The Limey* and *Sexy Beast* both play wittily, and sadly, with the past careers of celebrated older actors. On a literal level, the Limey is Terence Stamp himself, the Jeremy Irons of the 1960s, who plays the title role in the film. Stamp's former career as a movie heartthrob is reprised through one or two references to his role as Sergeant Troy in *Far From the Madding Crowd*, and through clips of an early film, *Poor Cow*, inserted into the text of *The Limey*. In *Sexy Beast* (which also stars Ray Winstone), Ben Kingsley perversely reprises, in an evil role, his famous performance in Richard Attenborough's English masterpiece, *Gandhi* (1982). Looking almost exactly as he did in that celebrated film of colonial India and contemporary guilt, Kingsley brings to the part of a villain the same concentration and fanatical zeal that made his Gandhi so convincing. The effect is of a parodic layering of historical moments. The saintly Gandhi flips over into the monstrous gangster Logan; the young Kingsley reappears weirdly in the willed intensity of the older man. But his brief visibility, while exhilarating, also asserts sadly the impossibility of return. And Ian McShane, a lost movie hero of the 1970s, appears as the solidification of a kind of shrewd, restless darkness. Always drenched by inescapable rain, McShane personifies London as the heart, energetic but bleak, of postmodern England. The Swiftian quality of theme and performance in *Sexy Beast* is striking. In an interestingly similar way, the actors chosen for the film of *Last Orders* are venerable performers, most of them with illustrious careers behind them. Some have appeared in films which captured definitively the styles and attitudes of different moments in British culture since the war. Michael Caine played a hero of Britain's colonial war in South Africa in the film *Zulu*. He went on to play a spy, Harry Palmer, in the classic Cold War drama, *The Ipcress File*. Tom Courtenay played Billy Liar in Schlesinger's famous 1960s film of that name. He also appeared in *The Loneliness of the Long Distance Runner* and the great romantic drama, *Dr. Zhivago*. A handsome bad-boy in the Terence Stamp mold, David Hemmings played the photographer in Antonioni's notorious *Blow-Up*, a definitive film of 1960s hedonism and angst. Helen Mirren has played a range of modern woman warriors, from the revolutionary Gosh Boyle in Ken Russell's *Savage Messiah*, to the heroic Jane Tennison in television's *Prime Suspect* series.

It remains to be seen how the fame of these actors and the resonances of their earlier roles will work together with the themes of loss, recollection, mortality, and immortality in the novel. Suffice it to say that at a moment in its history when England seems caught up in self-examination through various acts of remembering, the dramatization of a novel as replete with mourning and memory as *Last Orders*, seems perfectly apt.

5

Further Reading and Discussion Questions

This chapter builds on the preceding ones, framing questions for discussion and suggesting other reading. It is intended to open *Last Orders*, and Swift's fiction in general, to further study, and invite readers to wider exploration. The questions range from specific — addressing particular linguistic and narrative features — to quite broad in their historical, literary, and thematic scope. Many of the questions work closely with the reading of the novel I offered in Chapter 2. Others direct readers to aspects of the text suggested but not entirely developed there.

Swift and autobiographical writing.   We have seen that Swift believes in the power of the imagination to draw a novelist towards his/her full creative measure. He has spoken of the imagination as a magical mode of transportation, opening limitless possibilities to the writer willing to sacrifice the familiar and move into the unknown. In the light of these comments, we are struck once more by how different Swift's fictions are from each other, despite certain obvious similarities of theme and approach. How might we respond to the absence of clear autobiographical referents in Swift's fiction? Some of the writers who have influenced him drew extensively on their own lives for their material—James Joyce, for example. Others, like John Fowles, tend to avoid the explicit use of personal material. And readerly curiosity about what's "real" and what isn't in his fiction has certainly fueled the popular myth of Fowles as the enigmatic oracle of British letters. Is there an autobiographical imperative pressuring writers in our confessional age? What is the literary effect of Swift's avoidance of autobiographical elements? Has his status as a celebrity or the image of him as a kind of modern sage been affected by choices he has made in this regard?

Narrative point of view.   In his interview with Lewis Burke Frumkes, Swift stated his preference for the first-person narrative point of view, which gives him "that very intimate access to the character. And I like to write at the character's level, from the character's point of view." What are the effects of Swift's use of first-person point of view? Is this one of the ways in which he achieves intimate portraiture without resorting to autobiographical detail? What about the distance certain critics have perceived in his tone and approach to characters—is this erased or emphasized by the first-person p.o.v? As an exercise, compare and contrast two of Swift's short stories—"Seraglio," a first-person narration by a young man, and "Learning to Swim," which adopts the omniscient point of view. How does the use of voice in these two stories affect our perception of theme, character, and tone? Consider specifically the use of first-person narrative point of view in *Last Orders*: unlike *Waterland*, which is dominated by the voice of Tom Crick, *Last Orders* breaks up the first-person p.o.v., as it were, through the use of the interior monologue. How does Swift's technique here work to establish a sense of both individuality and collectivity?

Language. As we have seen, Swift has been both praised and criticized for his use of Cockney speech styles in *Last Orders.* Certain commentators have found Swift to be a fine ventriloquist, disappearing into the idiosyncratic language of his characters and thus paying them the compliment of independence, even from him. Other critics have found Swift's use of London vernacular and slang contrived and condescending. In the light of these differing opinions, consider the relationship between language and character, and between language and setting, in *Last Orders.* Does Swift's use of Cockney dialect lend authenticity to the novel, and if so, what kind of authenticity is this? On the other hand, does the language of the novel create an impression of falsity, as if the characters and settings were ethnographic exhibits placed on display for us in a sort of natural habitat? In a broader sense, could we see *Last Orders* — as well as Swift's other novels (especially *Waterland*) — as generating and "packaging" a picture of English life to be marketed to readers as a kind of nostalgic curio or tableau?

It would be useful, when investigating these issues, to compare Swift's representation of urban vernacular speech to Hardy's portrayal of the rural speech of his rustic characters. See, for example, *The Mayor of Casterbridge, Far from the Madding Crowd*, and *Jude the Obscure.* Faulkner's representation of the speech styles of the American South in *As I Lay Dying* suggests a clear point of comparison as well. By way of extending this question, consider *Last Orders* in the context of some recent films which emphasize the working-class English of the United Kingdom as a curious and even "exotic" language of its own. Examples here could include the movies of Roddy Doyle's novel *The Commitments* and Irvine Welsh's novel *Trainspotting; My Name is Joe* (which is subtitled in the manner of a foreign-language film, even though it's in English); *The Full Monty*; and *Sexy Beast.*

Thinking of language on a more specific level, consider Swift's admiration for what he sees as the down-to-earth, visceral properties of English: "Even without knowing other languages I am aware of the richness of English. The mixture of influences in the English language is marvelous. And it all comes together with this wonderfully concrete, physical Anglo-Saxon stuff." The example Swift chooses of a favorite word is "throb": "it is one of those words that simply sounds like what it is." Think about some of the themes of *Last Orders* in the light of these remarks: how is the novel's emphasis on the body and physicality reinforced by Swift's diction and vocabulary? List some specific examples from the novel. How does Swift reconcile his deep concern with spirituality in *Last Orders* with the blunt intensity of the language he so admires?

Swift's comedy. A number of the reviewers of *Last Orders* commented on the novel's humor, which was generally perceived as either rollicking and almost farcical, or graveyard-dark. Swift himself has attributed the comic energy of the novel to the interplay of character and situation — the ordinariness of the people depicted and the solemnity of the errand upon which they embark. Life, Swift says, keeps getting in the way of the four men seeking to honor their dead friend: "the life within the characters is tripping them up all the time, and that's where the comedy occurs, it's when life gets in the way of death." In the light of these diverse comments, consider the nature of Swift's comedy in *Last Orders*: is it slapstick, morbid, or some combination of the two? Does it relieve or add to the despair shown in the novel? How does the novel's humor contribute to the development of its themes, and enrich the narrative tonally and emotionally? The grim yet irresistible comedy of Faulkner, especially in *As I Lay Dying*, would again make an excellent comparison here. In addition, compare and contrast the humor of

Last Orders with the lack or minimizing of comic elements in Swift's other works — *Shuttlecock, Waterland,* or *Ever After,* for example. Compare and contrast Swift's comedy with that of other English novelists — deeply serious yet irreverent — with whom he might be linked: Evelyn Waugh, Muriel Spark, Julian Barnes, or Peter Ackroyd.

Place.   England itself — its identity, political future, historical role, and cultural mythology — is a vital actor, as it were, in Swift's fiction. We have seen how Swift may be closely associated with Ishiguro in his engagement with England as a place both geographical and historical on the one hand, and legendary or imagined on the other. Consider what kind of portrait of England emerges in Swift's fictions, especially in *Last Orders.* Is his England wholly imagined, as Ruth Pavey suggests when she describes Swift's Bermondsey as a "Bermondsey of the heart"? Or does he follow Hardy and Faulkner in mingling cultural myth, imaginative response, and physical fact in his portrayal of the country? Is Swift's England a cliché — of the romantic fenlands in *Waterland,* bustling London and the highly commercial southern coastal route in *Last Orders?* Do Swift's novels come across as "Masterpiece Theater" versions of England? Do they offer, that is, lush period detail and authentic accents in gorgeous Technicolor landscapes? Do they construct an objectified, even Disneyfied, England ready to be consumed by readers used to television and the films of Merchant-Ivory — readers whose historical sense has been conditioned by the pageantry of popular costume-dramas like *Elizabeth* and *Shakespeare in Love?*

On a less cynical note, Swift may be compared in this regard to other novelists who focus on England itself as a theme. E. M. Forster's "condition of England" novels, like *Howards End* and *A Passage to India,* as well as D. H. Lawrence's portrayals of the English landscape, would be illuminating here. Both Forster and

Lawrence evince a rueful nostalgia for a lost, ideal England which their fictions try to revive through the potentially transcendent energies of, respectively, spirituality and sex. Evelyn Waugh's fiction also sees the country as a kind of lost continent; *Brideshead Revisited* describes pre-war England as an Arthurian place, "irrecoverable as Lyonnesse." Do Swift's fictions reiterate or question this nostalgia — and if so, how? Alternatively, might we more accurately link Swift less to modernist romanticizations of England than to postmodern debunking of nostalgic myths? Does Swift parody nationalist yearnings, like Fowles does, or does he revive and celebrate them?

Relative to these issues, some useful works on contemporary fiction are Steven Connor's *The English Novel in History, 1950–1995* (1996), Michael Wood's *The Children of Silence* (1998), and Julian Wolfreys's *Being English* (1994). Anthony Easthope's *Englishness and National Culture* (1999) takes up the question from the broader perspective of cultural studies. For various explorations of nationalism from postcolonial angles, see for example, *The Post-Colonial Question* edited by Iain Chambers and Lidia Curti (1996), *Postcolonialism* by Ato Quayson (2000), *Migrancy, Culture, Identity* by Iain Chambers (1994), and *Colonial & Postcolonial Literature* by Elleke Boehmer (1995).

Swift and gender. Swift's depictions of women have drawn divided responses from readers. It seems hardly accidental that the field of Swift scholarship has thus far been dominated by men. In fact, gender is seldom treated as a theme in critical examinations of Swift's fictions. It is, though, crucially important, as we have seen. Female characters are often held at a distance from the reader, and their stories are tightly bound up with those of the men, who tend to control narrative in Swift's oeuvre. Narrative power itself is usually a masculine power, although women will sometimes be storytellers themselves. Helen Crick, Tom's mother in *Waterland*, is an example of a story-telling woman, and Tom attributes his love of stories and faith in their consoling power to Helen. Women are also, in a way, the originary ground of stories, for their bodies are the hatcheries of history, cause-and-effect, and plot. But in the novels before *Last Orders*, women seldom occupy positions of power as narrators. Sophie, who shares the narrative spotlight with various others in *Out of this World*, is specifically identified as ill; she narrates as part of the therapeutic process of psychoanalysis. Interpretive power over her narrative accrues effectively to Dr. Klein, her psychiatrist.

Furthermore, women tend in Swift's fiction to "tell" their stories through other than narrative means. They avoid claiming the power of the word, and "speak" themselves in indirect though highly traditional ways: through caring for or manipulating others (mostly men), and, especially, through producing children. The child often becomes an embodiment of (or substitute for) the woman's story in Swift's novels. Dick Crick expresses in himself all the tragic contradictions and losses of his mother Helen Crick's history. June Dodds similarly personifies Amy's story, and Sally Tate's lost baby sums up the directionlessness and canceled possibilities of her life. Usually, the woman who has miscarried or aborted a child finds herself mute, existentially compromised, and liable, in some strange way, to disappear from the text. Thus Mary Crick, sterile after a disastrous abortion, becomes more ghostly as *Waterland* proceeds, until Tom (and the reader) loses sight of her entirely by the end. In these ways, Swift's women characters utter themselves through their bodies rather than through their voices, and gravitate to the conventional female roles of mistress, muse, mother, and crone.

Discuss Swift's portrayal of women, considering whether he might be called an anti-feminist writer, or merely one interested primarily in masculinity and male experience. What are we to make of the treatment of abortion in his novels? Bear in mind here Swift's preference for male protagonists and narrators. With regard to *Last Orders*, consider whether the interior monologue liberates, in a sense, the female voice, and whether the novel suggests any shifts in Swift's engagement with women and gender. Some works of feminist criticism might be useful to consult here. For example, *Feminism/Postmodernism* edited by Linda J. Nicholson (1990), and *Sexy Bodies: The Strange Carnalities of Feminism*, edited by Elizabeth Grosz and Elspeth Probyn (1995). Judith Butler's *Gender Trouble* (1990) and *Bodies that Matter* (1993) offer complex readings of femininity as a physiological and cultural sign. Ato Quayson's chapter in *Postcolonialism*, entitled "Feminism, Postcolonialism and the Contradictory Orders of Modernity," is challenging, while Catherine Belsey's *Desire: Love Stories in Western Culture* (1994) approaches gender in the specific context of a literary genre.

Influences. Explore in more detail the interrelationships among Swift and some of the writers who have influenced — and continue to influence — him. Those discussed in Chapter 1 could provide a starting point here, and a springboard for thinking of others. In particular, consider Swift's engagement with the Bildungsroman (novel of education) as a genre, and discuss further his involvement with Charlotte Brönte (*Jane Eyre*), Dickens (*David Copperfield* as well as *Great Expectations*), George Eliot (*The Mill on the Floss, Middlemarch*), Joyce (*Ulysses* as well as *A Portrait of the Artist as a Young Man*), and Evelyn Waugh (*Brideshead Revisited, A Handful of Dust*). Think about Waugh also as a novelist who deals with spiritual matters; are there links between him and Swift in this regard — or between Swift and Muriel Spark, or Swift and Jeanette Winterson? Faulkner's influence on Swift's work is obvious, but consider whether it shows any resemblance to that of a younger

American modernist, F. Scott Fitzgerald. Does Swift rework in some ways Fitzgerald's evocation of a lost world in *The Great Gatsby*, or his portrayal of thwarted love in *Tender is the Night*?

Along similar lines, think more about Shakespeare as an influence on Swift. For example, does Shakespeare's vision of history in the history plays resonate with Swift's? Is there a hint of *Anthony and Cleopatra* in Swift's depiction of middle-aged passion in *Last Orders*? Swift's involvement with poetry is also fascinating. I have mentioned the echoes of Tennyson, Hopkins, and T. S. Eliot in his work. We might also trace the influence of W. H. Auden in Swift's preoccupation with the interplay between personal life and global upheaval, and in his sensitive treatment of masculine pain and joy. Ted Hughes's poetry informs Swift's work — generally, in Swift's vividly intense descriptions of nature and his lyrical passion for language, and with breathtaking specificity in the eerie image of the pike which appears near the end of *Waterland*. Interestingly, Hughes was, and Swift is, a fisherman.

Consider the comments which Swift himself has made on his influences. In the interview with Frumkes, he described a writer's influences as eclectic and haphazard: "The truth is that everything a writer reads influences him: the great, the good, the bad, and the ugly." While claiming influence to be often an unconscious process, he specifically identified Isaak Babel, a modernist writer of the 1920s and 1930s, as an influence. What traces of Babel might we find in Swift's fiction? Or, though Swift does not mention him, of L. P. Hartley, whose novel *The Go-Between* details the tragedy of a boy's loss of innocence — a basic theme in much of Swift's work? Do these relatively obscure writers emerge as more powerful influences than Swift's more famous "fathers," Hardy, Dickens, Joyce? If so, how might we account for this?

Finally, we saw in Chapter 1 how Swift's early reading gave him a strong sense of the word; but he has also said that as a child he did not read great works of literature: "They were the regular sort of kid stuff, boy's adventure stories." Does this "kid stuff" linger as an influence in his work, which deals so closely with boyhood and manhood, with the tension between adventure and the hearth? Might Swift be seen as the producer of "kid stuff" for grownups, writing the equivalent of Harry Potter stories for sad adults?

Age and death.   Swift's interest in boyhood informs his (sometimes parodic) reworkings of the Bildungsroman, as well as his deep pre-occupation with the Fall of humanity and the loss of primal inno-cence. Perhaps inevitably, such a concern with youth — its follies and passions, its terrible and unexpected suffering — requires a con-comitant concern with age. As for T. S. Eliot, Evelyn Waugh, and Kazuo Ishiguro (Swift's most Eliotian and Waugh-like contempo-rary), Swift realizes themes of loss and the passage from youth to experience through memory. For Swift, the obsessive memory of an old man is a repository of narrative authority — even though what that authority might mean is open to question. In such a memory resides interpretive power: the knowledge required to shape, if not fully to understand, youthful experience. There is something of Eliot's Gerontion — "an old man,/A dull head among windy spaces" — in Swift's curmudgeonly protagonists, who are both en-chanted and infuriated by history's "cunning passages, contrived corridors and issues." Gerontion's voice could be that of Tom Crick: history "gives when our attention is distracted/And what she gives, gives with such supple confusions/That the giving famishes the craving." Or, in the language of Ray Johnson, "It don't help you much, having been at the battle of El Alamein."

For Swift, memory is made paradoxically potent by age — by its bereaved but still-ardent energies, and by their distillation into a mixture of regret and hope. In the face of such bitter fervor, death appears often in Swift's work as both a consoling partner and an untimely phantom. Consider the motif of age and the importance of older characters in Swift's fictions; how do age and death relate to each other in his novels? What are we to make of those who die young—like Willy Chapman's wife in *The Sweet-Shop Owner* or Helen and Dick Crick in *Waterland*—or miss their chance at life, like Tom and Mary's baby, or June Dodds? Is there a unique vitality to the aged, especially in *Last Orders*? This question can be extended into an investigation of inter-generational relationships, the passage of time, and the vexed question of inheritance in Swift's work.

Interviews and websites. Published interviews with Swift may be found at the following locations: with Patrick McGrath in *BOMB*, Winter 1988–9; with John Kenny Crane in *Cimarron Review*, July 1988; with John Benrose in *Maclean's*, 6 May 1996; with Catherine Bernard in *Contemporary Literature*, Summer 1997; with Bettina Gossman in *Anglistik-Mitteilungen des Verbanes deutscher Anglisten*, September 1997; with Lewis Burke Frumkes in *Writer*, Februaury 1998. On the web, an interview with Swift may be found at *www.salon.com/weekly/swift-960506.html*. A website for Graham Swift at *http://landow.stg.brown.edu/post/uk/gswift/gsov.html* offers details on his life and work, and links to other kinds of information.

Bennetts, Melissa. Rev. of *Last Orders*. *Christian Science Monitor* 89:64. April 27, 1997.

Benrose, John. "A Long Day's Journey into Life and Death." Rev. of *Last Orders*. *Maclean's* 109:19. April 6, 1996.

Bose, Claire. Rev. of *Last Orders*. *Europe* 364. March, 1997.

Bowman, James. Rev. of *Last Orders*. *National Review* 49:4. March 10, 1997.

Bernard, Catherine. "Dismembering/Remembering Mimesis: Martin Amis and Graham Swift." In Theo D'haen, ed. *British Postmodern Fiction*. Amsterdam: Rodopi, 1993.

Cooper, Pamela. Imperial Topographies: The Spaces of History in *Waterland*. *Modern Fiction Studies* 42:2 (1996): 371–96.

Davenport, Gary. "Despair in Literature." Rev. of *Last Orders*. *Sewanee Review* 105:3 (Summer 1997): 440.

Frumkes, Lewis Burke. Interview with Graham Swift. *Writer* 3:2 (1998): 19.

Higdon, David Leon. "Double Closures in Postmodern British Fiction." *Critical Survey* 3:1 (1991): 88–95.

Ingelbien, Raphael. "England and Nowhere." *English: The Journal of the English Association* 48:190 (1999):33–48.

Irish, Robert K. " 'Let me tell you about' Desire and Narrativity in Graham Swift's *Waterland*. *Modern Fiction Studies* 44:4 (Winter 1998): 917–34.

Lehmann-Haupt, Christopher. "The End of Jack, or What Makes a Man Humble." Rev. of *Last Orders*. *New York Times*. April 11, 1996.

Lord, Geoffrey. "Mystery and History, Discovery and Recovery in Graham Swift's *Waterland*." *Neophilologus* 81:1 (1997):145–63.

McKinney, Ronald H. "The Greening of Postmodernism: Graham Swift's *Waterland*. *New Literary History* 28:4 (Autumn 1997): 821–32.

Parini, Jay. "Canterbury Tale." Rev. of *Last Orders*. *New York Times Book Review*. May 5, 1996.

Pavey, Ruth. "Heart of Bermondsey." Rev. of *Last Orders*. *New Statesman and Society* 9:386 (1996): 37.

Reynolds, Oliver. "On the Old Kent Road." Rev. of *Last Orders*. *Times Literary Supplement*. January 19, 1996.

Tredell, Nicholas. "Feelgood Fiction." Rev. of *Last Orders*. *Oxford Quarterly* 1–2:4–1 (Spring 1997): 37–41.

Widdowson, Peter. "Newstories: Fiction, History and the Modern World." *Critical Survey* 7:1 (1995): 3–17.

Bibliography

1. Works by Graham Swift

Fictions:

The Sweet-Shop Owner. London: Allen Lane, 1980.

Shuttlecock. London: Allen Lane, 1981.

Learning to Swim. London: London Magazine Editions, 1982.

Waterland. London: Heinemann, 1983.

The Magic Wheel: An Anthology of Fishing in Literature. Ed. Graham Swift and David Profumo. London: Heinemann, 1986.

Out of this World. London: Penguin, 1988.

Ever After. London: Pan Books, 1992.

Last Orders. London: Picador, 1996.

Miscellaneous:

An Interview with Kazuo Ishiguro. BOMB 29 (Fall, 1989): 22–3.

An Interview with Caryl Philips. BOMB 38 (Summer 1997): 32–5.

2. Select Criticism and Reviews of Swift's Work

Banville, John. "That's Life!" Rev. of *Last Orders. New York Review of Books,* April 4, 1996.